Copyright © 2019 Tekkan
Artwork Copyright © 2019

All rights reserved.
First Printing, 2019
ISBN 978-1-7343510-2-6

To contact Tekkan please email:
buddhaboy1289@gmail.com

Table of Contents

Everyday Mind VI . . . . Page 1

Galveston . . . . Page 100

Everyday Mind VII. . . . . Page 106

Waiting and Loving . . . . Page 196

Everyday Mind VIII. . . . . Page 207

Vietnam . . . . Page 298

Everyday Mind IX . . . . Page 309

Google and Facebook . . . . Page 388

Aslan . . . . Page 396

Appearances . . . . Page 407

Everyday Mind X . . . . Page 415

Transitions . . . . Page 498

Snap Shots . . . . Page 507

Introduction

I am an ordinary guy living a middle class life. I may imagine what it would be like to put on a wingsuit and jump off a mountain, but my stock-in-trade is the exploration of "everyday mind." I look for transcendent meaning in the ordinary happenings of daily life. I write in the morning everyday, and try to distill experience down to essentials. It is easy to overlook the instant-by-instant process of seeing, thinking, and responding to life — but in reality that is what life is.

The mind is self-interested and driven by powerful emotions. I look around and determine what to do. I judge what's worthy, and establish a list of priorities. My likes and dislikes become signposts, and if I am not careful I find myself repeating a pattern of behavior, and get stuck, narrowly seeing, feeling, experiencing — and then where is novelty?

Spring has sprung but today is chilly. I love watching the seasons change in a succession of little details, because the seasons are so much bigger than what's going on in my mind. There is always a lot going on in nature, and my practice is to open, so that more of reality may penetrate my consciousness.

I practice opening my awareness to the world inside and outside of me. Consciousness is a miracle — but I have to learn how to use the gift of Consciousness. This is what my poetry is about.

How to Read My Poems

I have married the sonnet to the tanka. I tell a story in the sonnet — using three quatrains, separated by line spaces, and a final couplet. The story builds to a conclusion in the couplet. The tanka is a commentary, or a counterpoint, to the sonnet — the combined poems have two endings.

I don't rhyme my sonnets, because I want freer expression. I want to be direct in my meaning — I want people to clearly understand my meaning. The metaphors are inspired by Shakespeare, and the (aimed-for) precision is in imitation of Japanese style. Using the sonnet with the tanka, I am mixing the sensibility of the Occident and the Orient — which I have done by living in England, Japan, and America.

I don't punctuate much in my poetry. I want the words themselves to do the work. There is logic between words, and the forms provide structure. By not using punctuation I hope to direct readers to carefully attend to each word — to appreciate the graininess of words.

Reading my poems silently, say, on a bus, a train, or an airplane, and reading them aloud, may be different experiences. The way I've written there's not always a pause intended at the end of the line. Hint: *My poems are to be recited not as lines, but as phrases, and a phrase often overflows the break at the end of a line. I pause and take a breath where it seems natural for me to pause. Another person may pause differently than I do.*

Each single poem is a piece of a mosaic, and it is my hope that the collection of poems form an accurate portrait of consciousness.

My daughter, Jocelyn MacDonald, is a wonderful artist. Her art work graces this book.

— *Tekkan*

Everyday Mind VI

Crumpled leaves are
accumulating
on the ground but
my cottonwood is
holding to the last.

Cold Mountain was a Chinese poet who
Wrote his poems on rocks and walls who lived
In a cave within hiking distance of
A Zen temple and people remembered

Him for over a thousand years because
His words are testimony of a life
Given to clouds and mountains and streams and
Meditation as he turned away from

Ordinary frustrations — and we don't
Know whether persecution or failure
Moved him to abandon society
But he cultivated his detachment

To surrender what he had left behind
And to savor the wind passing in pines.

He lingered over
the imperial consorts
of the capital
remembering beautiful
girls enfolded in brocade.

I'm not liberated like Cold Mountain
I haven't left society behind
My wife did leave me but then she returned
We aren't married but nothing else has changed

And I'm still publishing a journal of
Political opinion attending
To bitter controversies without end
As a partisan for liberty so

Half my time is devoted to a cause
And then I'm chasing enlightenment too
Which causes me nothing but frustration
So I am one mixed up *bodhisattva*

Is it necessary to abandon
Society and become a hermit?

My post office box
is my *dana* bowl
everyday I
depend on
donations.

During the hours of a day I am
Capable of being different people
As I appreciate waking up and
Allowing my thoughts to bubble and pop

And when I assume the lotus posture
I generate vigorous energy
So mornings are filled with optimism
And watching the sunrise is glorious

But by afternoon my vibrancy goes
As I dwell on the flow of money or
I get entangled in my opinions
And if difficulties become puzzles

It's possible to question everything
About my yesterdays and tomorrows.

I gain direction
from the might of morning
optimism and
practice circumspection and
tenacity later on.

Words on paper have no meaning if they
Are folded together in a book and
Gathering dust on a shelf even if
They are famous words that everyone could

Recite because communication needs
To be fresh as if you were giving me
A gift and I were holding it in my
Hands and nothing were more important at

The moment — because words are capable
Of resonance across time and space if
I absorb them with my being — because some
Words are authentic and are founded

On experience — and it's possible
I could awaken and live differently.

I am always here
though I am often
dividing myself
by doing two things
at the same time.

When I see half the leaves are on the ground
And the trees are gold red and yellow when
I see the white birch in its glorious
Yellow I want the season to stop and

Linger while the air is mild if only
For a week but I suppose that's the point
Of poignancy — there is no standing still —
There are only consecutive thresholds

And not everyone is present — but even
As I mark the turning year by raking
And bagging leaves even as I engage
In exhilarating activity

I can savor my wholehearted effort
And forget myself doing simple chores.

I pretend every
leaf is a lifetime
of experience
of best intentions
of transitions.

Larry is not conventional and he
Said he has twenty-eight knuckles in his
Hands and the same number in his feet so
All together he enjoys fifty-six

And then he said he has mountains in his
Hands which made me ponder my body and
Whether I have a river in my spine
A burning star in my stomach and an

Ocean in my ears and maybe my mind
Contains the entire universe as
Well as the emptiness that the stars are
Expanding into as everything is

Flowing outward after the Big Bang and
Maybe I'm a particle and a wave.

Dimensions of
reality
flow into me
but can I choose
what's coming out?

I could drift away with the clouds and get
Nothing done and it's easy to think of
Sailors in clippers who relied on block
And tackle on rope and sails to catch the

Wind or to think of farmers on tractors
Plowing their fields who spend lifetimes
Exposed to the sky who labor under
The mixture of light and shadow — but there

Is nothing to grasp and everything is
Fleeting — even though people attended
Carefully and categorized the types
Of clouds and invented names — just try to

Remember tomorrow how the clouds look
Now — and see if your memory is good.

Cirrus
cumulus
cirrocumulus
cumulonimbus
a halo around the sun.

Money is necessary to maintain
The building and to pay the salaries
At the Clouds in Water Zen Temple so
The board of directors initiates

The spring and autumn fundraising campaigns
And a pitch for donations is part of
Every Sunday service and the temple
Requires careful accounting because

We aren't separate from society and
The message of seeing directly in
To the mind and infusing this instant
With as much poise as possible so that

Whatever I do I'm appropriate
Needs a foundation of dollars and cents.

I presume the
frustrations of
earning a living
are included in
everyday *Dharma*.

The Plymouth Voyager

If sentimentality is a sin
I don't care — in remembering how Dad
Was learning not to drive anymore by
Smashing this van through the garage wall twice

In remembering the many times that
Joshua failed his driving tests and how
Inheriting this mangled van was his
Reward for success — in remembering

The many years I drove this Voyager
To Oakaboji and Spirit Lake in
Iowa with my parents my wife and
Kids for our annual vacation so

The natural ending of the van by
Corrosion is a cause for remembrance.

The familiar perch
behind the steering wheel is
like a captain's seat
from which I saw the clouds wind
turbines and cornfields pass by.

He was friendly and persuasive saying
The van was made in the year 2000
Which is unfortunate because in the
Next year Plymouth abandoned the faulty

Mitsubishi engine with a better
Motor which was bullet proof and on this
Voyager the components of the tires
Are only steel and not aluminum

Which would have been more valuable and
He chained the front axle and tilted the
Bed of the tow truck hoisted the van with
An irresistible winch and anchored

The van with chains and he said with regrets
He could give me only fifty dollars.

I spent the fifty
dollars on twenty-eight cans
of cat food because
that's the treatment for Johnnie's
urinary obstruction.

I'm happy my daughter Jocelyn and
Son-in-law Eric have relocated
To Stillwater from Philadelphia
Because instantly I have family

And now my refrigerator is full
Of grapes and concentrated grape juice and
Cheese and meat — and dinners left over from
Yesterday that I decide not to eat

Because they don't belong to me — but on
Halloween they carved pumpkins and spread the
Seeds on tinfoil and a baking pan and
Sprinkled on seasoning and poured over

Worchester sauce and roasted them in the
Oven and days later I swallowed them.

Not the doughnuts
not the cheese puffs
make me blink
but the pumpkin seeds
made me a criminal.

Because I'm smaller than most people I
Became a patron of thrifts stores where there
Is an oversupply of small-sized clothes —
And I bought four pairs of snakeskin — and a

Pair of alligator — cowboy boots — and
I have a closet full of silk and wool
Sports jackets — including the brand names like
Versace and Gucci and Harris Tweed —

And I have a rainbow selection of
Imported silk shirts from Asia — I live
In a prosperous community so
I have access to castoff luxury

That costs me practically nothing — but I'm
Stuck with the chore of lugging them around.

Fashionable
things make me
happy until
dissatisfaction
returns.

My daughter and son-in-law Erick are
Frustrated with me because I forget
To shut the lid of the toilet and their
Cat drinks the toilet water and I've been

Doing my best to remember and the
Point of meditating is to awake —
But yesterday I went to the bank to
Withdraw money to pay a handyman

And I divided the money into
An envelope and my wallet and I
Returned home and realized — I forgot
The envelope at the bank — so I raced

Back to the bank in frustration fuming —
And I found the money on the counter.

I can say — see —
I intend to be
good — but I am
trying to tame a
whirl-wind in my head.

I've heard doors slamming for more than thirty
Years and have grown accustomed to angry
Silences in the household and I'm passed
The confusion of assuming guilt that

Doesn't properly belong to me but
It remains difficult to move about
The bad feelings in the home — and the closed
Door serves as a protecting barrier

Between the two of us — that allows me
To see how trapped you are in your little
Room and how your anger that's hard to face
Is really just a façade that covers

Hurt that does not go away — and at heart
Your wounds from childhood are still festering.

I've learned to balance
powerful emotion with
a dispassionate
practice of meditation —
but you won't accept my help.

An empty sky and bare branches on a
Winter morning appeal to me as the
Sun casts itself on a landscape that's been
Drained of so much vibrancy — because the

Walls of homes the white fence and the crumpled
Leaves on the grass are drenched in a yellow
Light imparting a sense of cheerfulness
Even though the air is penetrating

And the trees are frozen in time — life is
Persisting and I enjoy the force of
The wind moving the needles and branches
Of the pine tree battering me about

My face and bare hands — and the trees may sleep —
But I have to keep moving to stay warm.

A blue sky appears
the same in any season
but the bare trees cast
shadows in a yellow light —
on an earth of drab colors.

I see an overcast sky differently
Once the leaves are down and a dusting of
Snow is on the ground and there's already
Ice on the sidewalk as I get to the

Coffee shop to meet my friends as we've
Gathered together for years — the covering
Clouds mark the threshold of winter but I
Also see the clouds are glowing with light —

And the glow is encouraging as we
Are cultivating enthusiasm
With conversation — and David shows me
A photo a man who was one of

Our group ten years ago and I see he
Fell into a hole in my memory.

I didn't forget
purposely but in
remembering
otherwise
he vanished.

The squirrel jumping between the branches
Of the bare trees in the pale morning light
Of November isn't comparing the
Day's temperature with summer — and it

Doesn't measure the quantity of light
As it's going about the business of
Living even as it has to scramble
To stay warm and fed — but now that the leaves

Are down I can see the squirrel easily
And I can absorb the stillness of the
Season and I can feel the weight of the
Arrival of winter again — and it's

Difficult to escape a measuring
Fear — because life is unpredictable.

Intelligence is
a gift and a curse —
as I can control
so much of my life —
but not everything.

When we meditate together I take
The lotus posture with a straight back and
With crossed legs and I become a breathing
Statue and my breath is inaudible

And as the time passes and energy
Builds my mind becomes a bowl burning all
My thoughts away until I can almost
Forget who I am and I become a

Bubble floating in emptiness but then
Sometimes my throat gets itchy or my nose
Begins to tickle and I swallow to
Suppress a cough or I twitch my nose to

To keep from sneezing but whatever I
Do I just can't prevent an explosion.

I don't want to
be disruptive
but I'm prone
to leakage and
eruption.

When I was a student I tried for an
Hour to describe the way the mown grass smells
In the heat of the summer and I searched
For appropriate words and phrases but

Was finally frustrated because I
Didn't know that the best words were
The names of the things themselves because
The names evoke the experience of

Seeing and smelling and absorbing — and
If you've never heard or seen the water
Flowing over rocks in the woods — when the
Leaves are down and the sky is overcast —

There are no words that can imitate the
Experience of a musical creek.

I used to cloister
myself within study rooms
with a desk and chair
with the walls painted grey
waiting for inspiration.

Year after year the branches return to
Bareness and bring recognition that the
Frost on the roofs and the cold are here for
The duration of winter and the breeze

That was gentle on my face is now sharp
And burns and the multiplicity of
Leaves sighing in the wind is replaced with
A howling or with a stillness that makes

Me imagine the earth is spellbound and
So much that was lively is now absent —
And yet as I see the nakedness of
The branches extending in the grey sky

Diminishing to the most delicate
Of twigs I think of my capillaries.

A burning sun
a beating heart
endure
persist.

Once the cold arrives I resort to the
Thick socks and the insulated jacket
That covers my neck with fabric and I
Wear a wool beret and put on my boots

And when I open the door I'm prepared
For the blast — I leave the car running and
Retreat inside to pour coffee into
Two large thermoses — because life without

Coffee would be meaningless — and then I
Have to put on my wool mittens again —
And turn the doorknob and open the car
Door while holding the thermoses all the

While wearing these thick things on my hands that
Minimize my finger dexterity.

I could put down the
thermoses or remove my
mittens but I like
unlocking the office door
in a flourish of bother.

I'm grateful the journal I'm publishing
Is in difficulty and I don't know
If can pay myself — and I'm thankful
My bills are accumulating — and that

Yoshiko's diabetes and cancer
Are a weight on my mind — because I've been
Muddling along without addressing
The fundamentals of my life and now

That complexity and befuddlement
Have come together while I possess the
Energy of a young man I will throw
Away my dispositions that are not

Useful — and I'll harness the urgency —
To discover what can be accomplished.

Because my troubles
are accumulating and
I don't know what to
do — I'll look for direction
from within and from without.

Entering a temple and becoming
A monk was alluring but I had a
Wife and children to provide for — teaching
English to Japanese in Japan was

Unconventional but we thought our kids
Would do better in American schools —
Starting over in America by
Working for my Dad running a printing

Press editing a publication and
Sustaining a campaign for liberty
Energized me but the operation
Is insecure and my family needs

Stability — for most of the day I
Am inspired but I need more money.

Obstacles may be
opportunities
to evaluate
everything I do
and see what's vital.

Propaganda is flying in the air
And circulating the globe even to
The remotest places and people are
Capable of believing anything

If ideas are presented with flair
And people are accustomed to tribal
Allegiances as we search for a group
Within larger groups to create home

And I'm aware of groupings based on race
Or ideology or a sense of
Historical persecution leading
To a mentality primed for fighting —

I sample the membership messages
But it's difficult for me to commit.

I'm searching for
a consciousness
free of bickering
enclosing people
who are like-minded.

When I think about the people who were
Airbrushed from the photographs of Joseph
Stalin because they fell in disfavor
With the Soviet Union I wonder

Whether the brush dispersed a very fine
Spray of paint or whether in fact color
Was brushed over the person erasing
His personage and I am sure that the

Work was meticulous and demanded
Dexterity — and then I think about
The millions of people who disappeared
Who were airbrushed from the earth in brutal

Fashion erasing their existence in
The service of an ideology.

The reality
is people are capable
of such monstrous
evil while professing the
utmost benevolence.

I don't remember what moved me to ask —
And I can't remember the household chore
She was doing and kept doing — after
She answered — but when my mother said that

Everyone dies a vortex entered my
Life — as a black hole was introduced — and
I couldn't understand what it meant that
Everyone grows old and even children

Can disappear and I wondered for the
First time where will I go — that even my
Home and neighborhood and my parents could
Not protect me from the dread of a death —

I don't remember what I was doing —
But I do remember being afraid.

My knowledge
and imagination
bump up against
ignorance and
I also forget.

I've read sailors' tales of a squall on the
Horizon that raises a fury of
Wind and rain when they had to climb and furl
Their sails in a tumultuous ocean

But catching an early winter cold is
Less dramatic and more gradual with
A soreness arising in my back and
Chest with my throat becoming hoarse and my

Head suddenly dizzy — and I have to
Rise from bed and dress laboriously —
And the road I'm driving on doesn't roll
And tumble and the wind isn't howling

But the bare trees and the grey sky are here
And there is no escape in grumbling.

I'm here for the
duration of
the winter — an
able-bodied
Minnesotan.

I welcome myself on my return to
My chair and window and keyboard and screen
Where I watch the world and formulate words
Because it's marvelous to see with a

Clear mind and body liberated from
A cold appreciating energy
Resuming my routines when I notice
How heavy the handle of the coffee

Pot feels as it fills with water and how wide
Apart I place my hands on the steering
Wheel while gliding on the familiar streets
And how my pens and books and papers are

Just where I left them but there's a frosting
On the roofs — remarkable this morning.

I can turn my head
without discomfort
following a hawk
gliding under a
white sky.

There's not a straight line in the cottonwood
Not even one elegant curve as it
Stands revealed in the frosty air of
The morning a dangling monstrosity

Of crooks and crags far too numerous and
Much too irregular to remember —
And even though it's by my house where I've
Lived for twenty years it's impossible

To describe in detail except to say
Its trunk is wide — and it towers over
Every other tree — and it's roots broke my
Sewage pipe — but if I closed my eyes I

Couldn't accurately imagine its
Form because there's nothing to grasp hold of.

I see two large crows
alighting on the highest
branches opposite
each other establishing
a cottonwood battlement.

I admire guys with hairy faces
Who grow hair evenly without the gaps
Most men have who from the first day that they
Stop shaving and every morning when they

Look in the mirror can see a steady march
To masculine satisfaction — but for
Me I stagger through desolate days of
Scruffiness when I know I look awful

But I think of my cottonwood as a
Paragon of nature because there is
No symmetry and every inch and curve
And twig is uniquely twisted and that's

OK — so I stay away from mirrors
Until my beard becomes presentable.

It's been years since I've
started and I'm doing it
only because change
is intriguing — I want to
see how a white beard will look.

Winter is the time for watching squirrels
Because they are exposed in bare branches
And I can see them clamber up and chase
Each other while nothing else is moving

And sunrises are spectacular in
Winter because they light an otherwise
Bleak landscape with ruby and violet
And orange and yellow and winter is

A season for meditation when I
Can see through the naked trees and the air
Is crisp and the sound of a car on a
Street reverberates and I can use the

Clarity and the tranquility of
Winter to question what is important.

Nothing is idle
and everything is moving
according to its
nature but I can pause and
consider where I'm going.

There is a bubble of peace about me
Because I work alone in a quiet
Neighborhood where I can watch the sun rise
Every morning but a point comes in the

Day when I turn my attention to the
News and lately women are accusing
Famous and powerful men of abuse
And the everyday fascination with

Victims and villains and recrimination
Is consuming new personalities
And while there are victims and villains
And recrimination can be useful

The news is always a stew of gossip
Excited by daily accusation.

I am a human
animal susceptible
as people are to
the cauldron of gossip but
I know it's dispiriting.

The monks at *Hosshinji* in Japan shave
Their heads as Buddhists monks have always done
For more than a thousand years because they
Want to sever attachment to worldly

Concerns as they know hair is easy to
Admire — and that's also why the Zen Priests
Wear mostly black robes with a splash of brown
To signify the highest status — and

The graininess of the wooden *Zendo*
Where everyone meditates is left a
Natural brown that's easy to forget
In the quest for enlightenment so that's

Why the tall monk Daigaku took offense
When I ambled about in a blue scarf.

Disapprovingly
he approached to take
my scarf and tuck it
in my black sweatshirt
re-establishing peace.

I was a bit lackadaisical in
The rigor I was determined to use
In my practice of Zen detachment from
Worldly affairs and ten years ago

When I was making more money than now
I bought two large rings of the same design —
Of a roaring lion with a mane in
The shape of a circle surrounding his

Face — and the gold ring has a diamond mouth
And diamond eyes — and the silver ring has
An open mouth and eyes — and I used to
Wear the rings on my middle fingers but

Now they are an impediment to my
Typing and I seldom want to wear them.

The bulky rings
made typing
difficult so
I returned to
simplicity.

Once I know the impetus of anger
And experience the raw energy
Coming with a seething resentment that
Makes me a superman for a few hours

I realize a threshold is crossed — and
Afterwards I am exhausted and left
With an altered mentality with a
Poisoned point of view so difficult to

Escape — but once I experiment and
Speak kindly and behave gently I don't
Need my justifications and my gloom
Dissipates and forgiveness is easy —

I'm not grasping for enlightenment but
I do appreciate a quiet head.

So much anger
is floating about
society but
running away is
not a solution.

It comes in the windows and even through
The walls the minute the furnace takes a
Break from heating the home as we have drawn
The curtains and locked the doors but there is

No mitigation of the weight of the
Cold on a winter night in December
In Minnesota even though we passed
The solstice and daylight will get longer

Gradually we face the coldest days
Of the year so it's not just tonight that
Is bearing down it's the burden of our
Knowledge of the months coming and there is

No use in grumbling so I put on my
Thick socks and pile up the heavy blankets.

While walking around
during the daylight only
a little oval
including my mouth eyes and
nose is exposed to the cold.

Kit Cat knows where to go in the house to
Take advantage of circumstances and
Yesterday during the coldest day of
The year he was dozing on the fuzzy

Blanket on my bed in a morning beam
Of sunlight dreaming Kit Cat dreams and this
Afternoon he was on his back stretching
His front and back legs happily in front

Of the vent that channels the heat from the
Furnace into the bathroom that is the
Smallest and so is also the warmest
Room in the house and he rolled upon a

Comfy mat when he saw me and closed his
Eyes saying — look how I am relaxing.

He doesn't have to
shovel snow today
doesn't confront
the biting cold doesn't wield
a shovel and snow blower.

Kit Cat doesn't bother controlling his
Tail and it follows mindlessly but when
Sitting pertly he curls it around from
The right and when he is watching me

In a crouch while I'm washing the dishes
Sometimes the tip of his tail will flick to
The right and left and in the morning when it's
Time for brushing his tail goes up as he lopes

Away and sometimes I see him poised to
Pounce and his tail is tense and when he is
Wrestling with the other cats Johnny
Or Henry there isn't any grace as

His tail is whipping in a furious
Chaos unpredictable and jerky.

I don't detect a
reflection of
sophistication or
commiseration
in his tail.

I would have to be careful if I had
A long tail because it would give away
My secrets and if I were impatient
I'd be snapping it back and forth and if

Angry my hair would stand up and my tail
Would be stiff behind me and if I were
Afraid I would not dangle but I would
Look angry — yet if I were embarrassed

Or disconsolate I would droop — and if
Curious or excited there would be
Swishing and swinging and if perplexed I
Think it would be frozen but with people

Watching me I wouldn't think about it —
I would assume a jaunty confidence.

While sitting
in a chair I would
swing my tail around
from the left because
I am left-sided.

My knowledge of science informs me that
The oxygen molecules closest to
The candlewick are moving faster than
Molecules further off and the result

Is the candlelight in the dark — and the
Christmas tree is electrically lighted
And I am enjoying the Christmas tree
And the presents and the candle light and

I am remembering everything that
Happened in this tricky and exhausting
Year — the weariness and satisfaction —
And I think it is extraordinary

That such an elementary thing as
Combustion can inspire emotion.

Somehow particles
elements and molecules
create seasons and
families and
Christmas.

The below zero cold has a way of
Waking me up in the morning that is
More impactful than a fender bender
While driving on the slippery roads of

Stillwater but as I bundle up and
Protect my feet and hands and ears I am
Almost impervious to the hostile
Air as I'm stomping about the snow in

My boots — but it's the inconvenience of
Putting on and taking off everything
Day after day that gets to me as the
Chore is unavoidable unless I

Don't care a bit about leaving puddles
Of melted snow from my boots behind me.

Unlocking doors while
wearing mittens and
holding containers
of coffee is an
everyday chore.

After leaving the conversation at
The coffee shop after our Saturday
Morning meditation I intended
To write poetry but realized that

My cell phone was missing so I searched the
Office with no relief and rushed back to
The Zendo where I used it to keep time
But it wasn't there so I returned to

The coffee shop hoping to seize it with
No luck and on the way back to my desk
I remembered the phone was more than a
Year old and I could buy a new one for

Twenty dollars a month over two years
But there it was being charged on a book.

The whirlwind had
returned to my
head as I forgot
to do one thing
at one time.

New Year's Day

It is worth recognizing — worth overdoing —
The holiday celebration with the
Dropping ball in New York City and the
Fireworks in Sydney Australia though

From one point of view it's just another
Second minute hour day week and year
Parceled out as long as anyone cares
To notice — the frictionless motion of

The earth and moon goes on unconsciously —
But for us the sun appears to rise and
Set and for me it's helpful to muster
My energy in bursts of effort that

I can measure with segments of time so
I can focus on accomplishments.

The cold
is impossible to
ignore but I will
attend to what I am
doing now.

I have struggled and competed enough
And I have compared myself with others
And I don't know how to stop measuring
Myself — and feeling the ups and downs of

Competition — and so the Buddha's words
Are alluring and I am practicing
To forget myself and to monitor
The subtle tricks I use to reinforce

Identity but I also love to
Play with words and harmonize rhythm and
Meaning and I enjoy discovering
How much reality I can capture —

There are moments of spontaneous joy
When words and ideas come together.

The master said
awakening happens
instantaneously —
do one thing
at one time.

I was driving through Stillwater doing
A chore turning on familiar streets and
I noticed the sun appearing with a
Right turn and with a left turn there was

The early morning moon — and I was in my
Working mind following the streets and the
Turns of the city but the sun and moon
Kept popping up around a corner and

Seemed to follow me — the moon was looming
White but yesterday it was yellow in
The dark — and there in a window was the
Lively reflection of the sun shining

Gold and my eyes didn't hurt in lingering
Over the sight — and then I was driving.

The sun and moon are
unearthly beauty
everyone can see —
they enliven the
sky everyday.

There are a hundred things more important
Today and after sixty years of life
I know how to leverage my energy
To achieve the most productivity

But it's one of the indignities of
Living to discover when pulling on
My wool sock that a cuticle has grown
At the base of the nail of my little

Toe and it's irritating to feel the
Growth standing up and catching on the wool —
And until it's gone it will be like a
Stone in my shoe so I am going to scrunch

Myself to reach the toe with clippers and
Angle in carefully and cut it out.

In the scheme of life
I wonder what is
the purpose of a
cuticle that grows
on a little toe.

Kit Cat often jumps to the countertop
In the kitchen even though we push him
Off and scold him — he is determined and
Perhaps he feels dominant when he takes

A high position — and one day I was
Sitting on the couch in the living
Room within sight of the countertop watching
The television and Kit Cat knocked a

Container off the countertop and I
Heard it plop and saw him looking at me
Waiting for me to respond and I knew
He was manipulating me so I

Made of show of opening and closing
The drawers and I even turned a doorknob.

He stretched up
to move the knob
with his paws but
couldn't and I
said nothing.

Kit Cat is not like Johnnie and Henry
Who want me to brush them and when I sit
On the floor and call they come and Jonnie
Will even turn around for me to brush

The other side while Kit is watching from
A distance because he knows he's next and
From experience he knows if he hides
Behind the T.V. I'll grab him later

But he runs to make me chase and then I
Kneel with him before me and brush while he
Complains and afterwards he struts away —
But one day he seized the brush from my hands

And holding it with his front paws he nailed
It with his back paws and then scampered off.

Kit determines
how to respond —
he will not be
a docile follower.

To be awake and spontaneous in
A way that does not summon negative
Consequences I have to acquire
Optimism and persistence and I

Need to have transcended the grip of fear
That can so easily infect every
Aspect of my personality — as
I have learned it's useless to run from my fears —

It's better to recognize my fears and
Do what's necessary and base my faith
On the assumption that I am living
A life that never ends but does transform —

So whatever impediments arise
Before me are only ephemeral.

It's necessary
for me to transcend my fears
and to base my faith
on a persisting goodness
I can grow into.

So what does my spontaneity do
When a cold front is coming in behind
The falling snow with the expectation
Of the return of below zero cold

With my long underwear washed and ready
With my cold weather boots and mittens and
A hood attached to my jacket that makes
Me mostly invulnerable to the

Weather as I'm absorbing the gloomy
Sky and the bare branches and the drizzle
That will become a dump of heavy wet
Snow that I will be removing soon — how

Does spontaneity show itself on
A day when everyone just wants to hide?

I go about the
day as buoyant as if it
were a cloudless day
in summer realizing
the sun does make the clouds glow.

There is a saying that sticks in my mind
About a Zen master who asserts that
People he meets are not different people —
They are himself — and I'm not sure of his

Meaning and I can't quite make the jump in
Understanding to see as he does but
I often catch myself watching my friends
And acquaintances and my family

And I gauge their reactions to me as
If they were mirrors reflecting on my
Worthiness and even though I know what
I'm doing sometimes it's difficult to

Escape the weight of self-obsession so
I will put my faith in transformation.

Zen masters use
riddles that stick
in the mind like
a returning
itch.

When Zen people get together we like
To ring a bell to signify when it's
Time to enter the Zendo and begin
Our meditation and some people get

The urge to hit the bell for no reason
Except to hear it ring but as the guy
In charge I frown on unsanctioned ringing
So when Jane casually moved to strike

The bell I came behind her back and with
Her stroke I immediately pinched the
Bell and re-established the quiet — but
I failed to anticipate what Jane would

Do standing with a mallet in her hand
And she hit me — a thunk — on my forehead.

It is fortunate
I am not the guy in charge
of military
strategy as I fail to
think of probabilities.

If I were an angel liberated
From the disagreements and frustrations
Of everyday living there would be no
Possibility for growth on the earth

And I wouldn't feel misunderstood and
Separate and I wouldn't doubt myself —
Nor would I question everything — nor would
I experience fear — angels are dreams

Of the imagination and serve as
Emissaries for a goodness that is
Invisible and untouchable so
Often — but I have come to live for those

Days when I do something surprising and
Find satisfaction and liberation.

The things I do
have resonance
informing me of
consequence if I
attend carefully.

When I'm sitting quietly before dawn
There is nothing in the house to distract
Me from myself and that is when I get
To know the acrobatics of my mind

And there is always a choice whether to
Follow the direction of my thoughts and
Whether to become enamored of the
Emotion attached to my thinking or

To let the whirl-wind go and because a
Thought and the emotion connected to
The thought will take a natural amount
Of time as long as I'm not obsessing

I may practice holding up the bowl of
My mind — letting the bowl fill and empty.

I am the
emptiness
the emotion
passes through —
I am watching.

A car is a modern-day chariot
And a symbol of personality
That also serves as armor against the
Extremes of cold and heat and snow and rain

And when ensconced inside I listen to
The radio fascinated with my
Political controversies and when
Bored I turn to music stimulating

Pathways in my brain that make me vibrate
And someone is always driving slower
Than me and I can't pass or someone is
Behind me desperately wanting to get

Around and whatever's happening it's
Difficult to do one thing at one time.

Sometimes I turn
the radio off
and my thinking
is exposed.

January is January when
It gets as cold as it ever does in
Minnesota and doing anything
Outside is complicated like turning

Keys while wearing mittens and holding my
Two containers of coffee in the dark
And it's my fingers and toes and ears that
Need protecting while my nose is OK

But then there is the January thaw
When the snow on the driveway and sidewalk
And on the city roads too smears itself
Onto my boots and car and the sticky

Mess is everywhere and everyone leaves
Behind a trail of salty nastiness.

As a veteran
of winters I use
lotion on my
fingers and Lip Balm
to prevent cracking.

We don't refer to barometers or
Rely on eyewitnesses in the west —
We don't even have to watch the bearing
Of the clouds anymore because we have

Weather people broadcasting satellite
Images but in the morning with my
Group of sober alcoholics I said
The snow was late and everyone was wrong

Because when it snows an icon appears
On my phone of little white dots but now
There are solid black bars clearly meaning
We have escaped the snow again today

And Joe said I could be in denial
But momentarily we will know truth.

Spinning and swerving
I progressed about an inch
and had to shovel
again to clear my tires
because snow was everywhere.

There is no use in grumbling in the
Middle of a storm and I was lucky
To get my car in the garage before
The accumulating snow made driving

Impossible so I zipped on my one
Piece suit and chose the hat with ear flaps and
Tugged on my boots and prepared for battle —
And I pulled snow off the roof with a rake

And set the snow blower at the slowest
Speed and trudged forward spewing a steady
Stream and when the driveway was cleared I took
My shovel and proceeded to stab and

Fling along the walkway and was almost
Finished before my fingers were frozen.

I wear the woolen
mittens from an army
surplus store but
after a while my
fingers always freeze.

As I see the morning light painting the
Cottonwood orange and I notice a
Mountainous pile of snow bordering the
Street along my property things appear

As they should in January after
A snowfall and yet it seems I'm on a
Journey in a world of surprises and
Even though a heavy snowfall often

Happens and the city plows do what they
Always do and every winter I clear
The driveway and shovel the walkway
This morning my familiar neighborhood

Is hidden by a foot of the freshest
Snow under a blue sky showering light.

The lilac bush is
bare — the trees are brown but
my magnificent
cottonwood is reflecting
the glorious sun.

It's convenient to parcel out my life
In days and weeks because the rising and
The setting sun is easy to go by —
And if there weren't day interspersed with night

It would be much harder to remember
What I did last week — and I am really
Grateful for my eyes to see bare branches
In a blue sky and grateful for my skin

And body so I can know what the cold
Of winter is — and also there is my
Marvelous mind that reminds me while a
Chill is rising from the snow on the ground

In several months the roses bloom again
And in summer I may wear a t-shirt.

I see the moon in
the morning and in
the afternoon too —
it's an everyday
presence to go by.

When I understand nothing moves faster
Than light and that the light from distant stars
Traveled billions of years to reach the earth
Then I appreciate immensity

And when I understand that during the
Passage of the light the stars radiating
The light have imploded and no longer
Exist then I encounter mystery —

And when I consider that the forces
Of gravity are whirling galaxies
And everything that exists is moving
In relation to every other thing

Then I have to put my life and efforts
In context with a sobering cosmos.

I have questions
and would like
solutions but
also I love
a rising sun.

The light a star generates radiates
In all directions and on earth we see
The cosmos from a limited point of
View and I believe it's necessary

To question where we are going and to
Grasp purposes worthy of our living
Because we have the curiosity
And the wherewithal to comprehend so

Many of the facts about us and we
Know immensity and minuteness and
We understand our tininess within
The universe but no one can explain

How our molecules and electrical
Impulses create thought and emotion.

The immensity
of the cosmos is nothing
compared with the
everyday miracle of
ordinary consciousness.

I am a seeker of inspiration
And when confused or afraid or angry
I have had to practice patience because
Patience seems the best medicine in the

Middle of disagreement — and sometimes
The best I can do is not to express
All the anger within me but to leave
An argument unresolved and to let

People believe what they want about me
At least until circumstances change and
The unreasonable expectations
Anyone could have are recognized and

Sorted out — even sharp emotions can
Be useful if I can summon patience.

The morning after
an argument I
can cherish
justifications or let
emotions dissipate.

There is no predicting of the rewards
Coming from patient observation once
A time of day is set apart and the
Chattering of distracting thought is tamed

When I come to my desk at the same time
Everyday to find what is worthy of
Remembering today as I see the
Same ground and trees and houses that were here

Yesterday and sometimes disagreements
And angry words reverberate but now
There is a covering of snow and the
Crystals of snow are shining in the light

And the apple tree is slightly frosted
And the far horizon is blue and white.

Some days I don't
see the trees in
front of me
because words are
reverberating.

Some people claim to have mind palaces
Meaning they have the ability to
Store and recall the information they
Use efficiently and perhaps there are

Porticos and vestibules attached to
The ornate chambers of rumination
And maybe when a question arises
There is a salon where the various

Voices of opinion can debate and
I suppose that the most superior
Amble about with a structure much like
A gothic cathedral in their heads

But I struggle when tying my shoe to
Simply tie my shoe without distraction.

I was reversing
in a parking lot
and smacked into a
car that wasn't there
a moment ago.

The earth is turning on its axis and
Revolving about the sun and even
Our solar system is caught in a net
Of gravity so everything is in

Motion — and with my first sip of coffee
In the morning warmth coincides with the
Sunlight and optimism and play with
Words but in the afternoon energy

Dissipates and doubts and fears arise so
Every emotion is transitory —
Everyday I see the same branches of
The same trees and enjoy my rootedness

In this place even as I am gaining
Momentum and moving to mystery.

I protect myself
with repetition
but need to
leave room for
innovation.

A flame of consciousness is consuming
This moment considering everything
Evaluating priorities and
Preparing a response and I know how

Precarious my perceptions are and
How vulnerable I am to waves of
Combustive emotion because there is
A hunger for love and a fear that love

Is unobtainable as my thoughts are
Whispering I am not worthy of love
And I recognize the burning power
And I know such thinking is deluded

And believe many endure such thinking
So I will practice letting go of thought.

I prefer a
candle's radiance
but endure
lusty fire.

Cold Mountain followed the tradition of
The Chinese poets who left the cities
And roamed the country in solitude but
The river and mountain poets wanted

Their poems to be celebrated — Cold
Mountain rejected the snares and misery
And futility of civilized life
And he used the conventions the other

Poets did but he wrote his poems on the
Rocks and walls and trees with no intention
Of preserving them — and only through the
Efforts of others were they saved and passed

Down the centuries to show he was a
Poet who gave himself to expression.

In a dream a
woman with white
hair was looking
at him but did not
recognize him.

I meditate before dawn and meet with
Sober alcoholics for talk and for
Most of the day every day I have a
Clear head and am enthusiastic and

I practice composing words into lines
And search for appropriate words in good
Order and sometimes it's necessary
To start over again and sometimes I

Have to wait for a word to arise and
When it does it is recognizable
As a word worth waiting for on the way
To a couplet epitomizing a

Sonnet in which every word is correct
And the sonnet reveals simplicity.

The word arising
is a rediscovery
of what I already
knew but hadn't
yet signified.

The iron in my body came from an
Exploding star billions of years ago
And my body is composed of atoms
And molecules and strands of DNA

That testify to an origin I
Share with every living being on earth
And within my body there are layers
Of organization where cells behave

Independently and for the good of
The whole also so that I can sit at
My table and cut an orange into
Pieces and taste the taste of an orange

And I can speculate from this table this
Moment is moving to infinity.

There are billions
and billions of stars
in space and atoms
in my body — there is
also consciousness.

Scientists uphold a prism of glass to
Separate the light into colors and
They aim spectroscopes to see the colors
Of starlight and thereby they deduce the

The age and chemical composition
Of the most distant stars and in a few
Thousand years by working together they
Have exposed the swirling cosmos and the

Inescapable fragility of
Humanity too and yet our human
Comprehension resembles a super
Nova bursting and seeding the empty

Spaces with a consciousness that will not
Be satisfied with lingering questions.

Even before the
questions could be
formulated there was
cooperation — there were
words.

Drunks with my genetic disposition
Usually don't live to reach my age
But if they do they leave behind a trail
Of misery and misunderstanding

And recrimination because until
An alcoholic or a drug addict
Surrenders and embodies a power
Greater than himself and until he is

Reformed by invisible power and
Is encouraged by everyday friendship
With fellow alcoholics who are on
The same path the addict is a whirlwind

Because he and his family do not
Understand — he's lost control of himself.

Perhaps one in ten
can't stop consuming
drugs or alcohol
but there is power
and recovery.

A drunk's thinking is all mixed up and his
Whirling thoughts cannot be separated
From the urge to drink and by himself he
Is confounded — though he is blind to his

Predicament and sincerely believes
He is a victim of circumstances —
There is a powerful charge attached to
Thinking and emotion and a drunk is

Lost in suppositions while the drink used
To bring sanctuary and pleasure but
As alcoholism progresses the
Respite from misery vanishes and

There is no escape from isolation
And he slowly begins to hate himself.

Why doesn't he change
his attitude and reform
himself — is it so
difficult not to take the
first drink?

The descent into the desperation
Of alcoholic thinking comports with
The poison of alcohol but once the
Drunk has surrendered and becomes willing

To do anything for sobriety
She enters into the circles of light
Hearted conversation where she will find
Companions who share her experience

And she will be offered a process of
Recovery that cuts across the grain
Of ordinary self-reliance and
Points to an unspecified power of

Her interpretation that already
Exists but has been inaccessible.

Dead end
behavior is
exhausted and
new thinking is
possible.

The immensities of the cosmos and
The impersonality of the laws
Of physics don't matter that much to me
Nor do I care that for most of human

Experience there was no remedy
For the curse of alcoholism — the
Fact is I have been sober for more
Than thirty years by cultivating a

Faith in a power greater than myself
A power I am growing into based
On love and forgiveness and gratitude
And I believe whatever happens to

Me I will be OK even if I
Die because consciousness will persevere.

The cosmos may
expand forever with
dark mass and
dark energy
nobody understands.

The ancient Chinese were meticulous
But they lacked our accumulation of
Knowledge so they could not understand the
Behavior of an atom but the words

Of Zen monks transmitted through centuries
Testify that the rocks and grasses and
Mountains are moved by an unborn and an
Undying presence in everything that

Does not hurry and yet accomplishes
The sowing and the harvesting of the
Seasons in proper time and the river
And mountain poets of China aspired

To harmonize their passions with the cloud
Generating mountains and with the moon.

They cultivated
unflinching poise
uncompromising
receptivity
to whatever comes.

Can you see the questing spirit in the
River and mountain poets and in the
Solitary living of Cold Mountain
Exploring the wilderness of China?

They were the mandarins and keepers of
Tradition who became dissatisfied
With the exercise of power and who
Wanted to pursue the mysterious

Allure of nature by leaving cities
And experimenting with their bodies
With sensations and consciousness watching
And learning from the seasons attending

To the emergence and disappearance
Hearing the gibbons howling in the trees.

They applied
consciousness
and experience
distilling nature
in everyday mind.

I enjoy learning about the quirks and
Quarks of space/time but there was a foot of
Snow last night and I was too leisurely
About its removal from my driveway

And when I aroused myself the sun was
Beaming and the moist snow was clogging my
Snow blower and the realization
Came it was necessary to shovel

The imposing pile the city plow had
Left blocking my entrance and I had to
Slice the snow with the side of my shovel
To loosen it and then I had to make

A wide base to heap a mountain of snow
Upon at both corners of the driveway.

Snow accumulates
during the winter and can
only be piled to
a certain height and so
the mountains grow sideways.

It wasn't pleasant to realize I
Had to shovel the entire driveway
Because the snow was too wet and heavy
For the snow blower but my revulsion

Wasn't moving snow so after the pile
At the entrance was hurled to the sides I
Began to push snow with my shovel on
The asphalt and discovered the power

Of my hips and legs and momentum and
I forgot the driveway and walkway by
Just moving the bit of snow here and by
Indulging animal energy and

By pacing and after finishing I
Surveyed my driveway with satisfaction.

The snow continued
to melt but I took
a photo with my
phone to remember
the enormity.

I am taking time to look at the creases
Of my palms and to appreciate the
Many fine wrinkles they have grown into
And there are the insides of my fingers

That I'm flexing and then I turn my wrists
And see the blood vessels on the backs of
My hands and remember in a moment
I did unzip my jacket and hold the

Sides and pull the jacket off without a
Thought about how useful my hands are and
I realize that I constantly do
Hold and grip and pull and twist and turn and

Rub and caress and touch with the tips of
My fingers without appreciation.

The world is as it
is but I wouldn't know so
much if I couldn't
pick it up and hold it and
explore with my fingers.

A boxer has trained to get maximum
Impact into a blow and he imparts
Leverage coming from his legs and hips
And abdomen as force swells throughout his

Body and is focused in several
Knuckles and I believe he has fashioned
His spirit for the giving and taking
Of punishment and has cultivated

A personality for a contest
Of wills with a style of evasion and
Attack and a magic of motion that
Earns him a name and reputation but

I wonder whether the effort precludes
The opening of his gentility.

The warrior
stands on the earth
and the impetus of force
arises from the earth
and flows through his body.

A lover is like everyone and is
Distracted by a thousand details as
He goes about his days rushing to get things
Done but a lover is also awake

And takes the time to feel the grain of the
Wooden chest of drawers and notices the
Texture of the cotton undershirt as
He takes it out and puts it on and knows

Its lightness — and holds the steel container
Of coffee and weighs it in his hand and
Drinks closing his eyes and following the
Warmth going down and spreading out — even

On the busiest day it's possible
To appreciate the world in passing.

A lover's love
emanates from
unreasonable
unexplainable
gratitude.

Writing poetry is a method that
Generates enthusiasm and gets
Me out of bed and even my dreams
Are inspiration for poetry and

Usually I'm happy because of
My poems but there comes a time in the
Day for doing the work that generates
A paycheck by means of publishing a

Journal of political opinion
When I turn from the ethereal and
Become realistic and when I hear
People say regarding their opinions —

I follow my heart — I think we would do
Much better if you were more circumspect.

There is just too
much detail and
deception woven
in the framing of
political words.

When young and ignorant I watched my Dad
Engage in political writing and
Was repulsed by the severity of
His attitude but after observing

How politics is maneuvered it is
Manifest that the most effective ploy
Is to be smugly righteous and accuse
The other guy of inhumanity

And if the accusation is brief and
Easy to digest the facts don't matter
And the news people will cooperate
Because passion creates an audience

And it is propitious if the news
Media and the accuser agree.

Too often
politics is not
about solving
problems.

European revolutionaries
Figured out centuries ago that the
Way to manipulate the masses was
To use the obvious disparity

Common in societies divided
By class and to demonize the King and
The aristocracy and the bishops
And they circulated their pamphlets

On equality and liberty and
On brotherhood but they relied on hate
And violence and whatever good was
Intended was overwhelmed in a rush

Of accusation without mercy and
The usual use of a guillotine.

Revolutions are
made of zealotry
and revenge
not charity
or justice.

There are conspiracies behind doors and
In the corridors of the capital
In the best of times and the secrets and
The trading of influence the public

Doesn't see is justified because the
Conspirators are lawmakers who are
Expert at serving the public interest
With a show of articulate concern

And a wealthy nation has a heap of
Tax revenue to divvy up and a
Pile of regulating to do and the
Tax code is too complicated but it

Benefits the corporations that know
Whom to call and how much to contribute.

An exquisite
system of laws and
a balancing of powers
aren't quite enough
to compel compassion.

The Washington Correspondents Dinner
Is a black tie affair where the nation's
Top news personalities gather to
Celebrate their prominence because they

Comprehend the complexities at the
Apex of government and they serve as
Mediators for the ignorant and
The downtrodden and they exemplify

The better angels of America's
Conscience as it is necessary to
Remind our nation of historical
Misdeeds and we should have gratitude for

This collection of special intellects
For providing such gentle correction.

They are the
guardians of
democracy and
the library of
the law.

Does anyone remember Walt Whitman
Our loafing poetic American
Hero who discovered the cosmos in
A blade of grass who celebrated the

Exuberance of the nation he loved
A nation of heroes who constructed
The California Aqueduct and the
Empire State Building and the Hoover

Dam and who sent astronauts to the moon
But Walt Whitman also cared for and grieved
For the dismembered and dying soldiers
In our nation's capital during the

Civil War and he memorialized
American tragedy with his words.

Too many
Americans today
are ashamed of
America.

The Internal Revenue Service tried
To extinguish our publication thirty
Years ago by revoking our status
As an educational foundation

Because some small-minded bureaucrat was
Offended by our political point
Of view so they sent an agent with a
Mission to examine our books and my

Dad provided a chair and table in
The garage but he wasn't permitted
Inside the office and the I.R.S.
Failed ignominiously to stop us

When the governor of Minnesota
Responded and compelled them to retreat.

Throughout the
intrusion my Dad
continued to play
golf in the afternoon
at the club.

It is fashionable today to be
Skeptical and even a little bit
Suspicious of explicit displays of
Manliness and there are thinkers at our

Universities proposing that the
Usual views of male and female roles
Are outdated constructs of a worn out
World and we should be excited and be

Liberated with new alternative
Modes of being — and didn't we suspect
While watching the swaggering bravado
Of the clownish cowboy John the Duke Wayne

There was something exaggerated and
More than a little crazy about him?

We don't have to
be oppressed by
testosterone — we
can repudiate
toxic masculinity.

I didn't like my Dad for many years
Because he wasn't in tune with the times
When I was a teenager listening
To rock music and I didn't want to

Be seen with him as he was serious and
Aloof and embarrassing while I was
Dreaming of a separate world full of
Romance without his presence but looking

Back I perceive our home was orderly
And we had the necessities of life
And I believe it's not unusual
To turn away from the imposition

Of authority while at the same time
Relying on the protection he gave.

Now I know
from seeing wreckage
in America
boys are lost
without fathers.

The temperature at the core of the
Sun is ten million degrees and the force
Of gravity is fusing nuclei
Of hydrogen atoms together and

Producing helium and energy —
And it takes ten million years for the heat
And the light to percolate and emerge
At the surface of the sun — and it takes

Only eight minutes to radiate to
The horizon in front of my desk and the
Light illuminates craggy cottonwood
Bark and the light comes through the window and

Through my eyes into the synapses of
My brain empowering my consciousness.

The sun on my cheeks
originated ten million
years ago in the
core of the sun ninety
three million miles away.

When the snow is falling in tiny grains
At a rapid pace at the beginning
Of March with the temperature around
Freezing I know this is the type of snow

That accumulates and it's removal
Is tricky because it's wet and heavy
On the verge of melting and clogging the
Snow blower so in the evening I

Like to pull the curtains to the windows
And deny the snow is falling for a
While but in the morning I get to it
Before it's soggy and the moment I

Open the door and put my foot into
The snow I can gage the trouble ahead.

There is always
disharmony
with someone
that comes to mind
while I am moving snow.

Galveston — 1900

Galvestonians had no warning of
The hurricane howling and impending
And six thousand were lost on Sunday night
And debris covered the ground three miles long

And two stories high while the bodies of
The missing were swept out to sea but the
Survivors were left with the question of
Staying or abandoning the island

Fleeing the sticky sweltering summers
Saying good riddance to the mosquitoes
And mostly who would abide in a place
Where God had swept with a mighty hand and

Destroyed years of careful habitation
And they decided somehow to rebuild.

Starting over
someplace new
couldn't be done
because their roots
had taken hold.

The Seawall

Logs of yellow pine from Beaumont Texas
Were driven through the sand forty feet down
Into the clay — and concrete composed of
Crushed granite was layered over as a

Foundation reinforced with steel rods — and
Before the seawall was built giant blocks
Of granite from central Texas were placed
On an apron as a buffer from the

Bay — and granite of diverse sizes made
A riprap breakwater extending out
Twenty-seven feet — and a concave wall
Was raised in sections with the curve facing

The water — and a tongue and groove system
Connected pieces allowing movement.

Galvestonians
asserted a wall
seventeen feet tall
above a low tide
against coming storms.

The Galvestonians determined that
Five hundred square blocks of the city had
To be raised seventeen feet so they dug
A canal behind the seawall for the

Dredge boats from Germany and they lifted
Two thousand buildings onto stilts and the
Boats scooped the fill from the bay and by means
Of capacious pipes a mix of water

And sand was pumped into place while the pipes
Were continuously repositioned
And people moved about on hoisted
Boardwalks and by street cars running on rails

That were doggedly reconfigured and
Finally Galvestonians were done.

The engines of the
dredge boats pumped mostly water
but grain by grain of
sand settled in place until
the town was elevated.

St. Patrick's Catholic Church had the panache
Of a European cathedral — a
Stone structure of monumental heft with
A tower and stained glass windows — that had

To be raised so the Galvestonians
Employed one hundred laborers who turned
Seven hundred jackscrews one half inch at
A time and over thirty-five days they

Raised the church five feet and poured a concrete
Foundation and the feat was accomplished
Without cracking the walls while services
Continued without an interruption

Showing that faith and ingenuity
Can in deed move a mountain of limestone.

Not everyone
believed the deed
could be done but
some had to be
optimistic.

Electricity was coming and they
Used steam engines for dredging but they lacked
The accumulated industrial
Might that prepares people today to raise

Towers in the sky so they relied on
Ingenuity determination
And faith in rebuilding Galveston not
So differently from the Egyptians who

Generated the pyramids — and in
1915 a hurricane stronger
Than that of 1900 assaulted
The island and inflicted terrible

Damage but only six people were lost
And the Galvestonians persevered.

It's peculiar
and quite human
to put down roots
on a sand island
exposed to hurricanes.

I choose to believe
irritations are
thorns on the way to
metamorphosis.

Direction and
propulsion are
manageable
while emergence is
unpredictable.

— *Tekkan*

Everyday Mind VII

Snow is melting and
water is flowing
downhill across the
streets of Stillwater
and joining the river.

This is the time of the husk of winter
When snow is melting in the afternoon
And freezing again overnight so that
There are puddles on my driveway that I

Step around to keep from getting my shoes
And socks wet during the day and yet I
Could slip and fall on the early morning
Ice — and as I'm driving about town there

Are piles of towering snow bordering
The parking lots of Stillwater that are
Gradually disintegrating and
Every year I mark the progress of their

Disappearance as the arrival of
Spring while sunlight is generating strength.

Downhill from my house
on the south side of
the street under a
shady pine every
year the last snow melts.

The dawning light through the stained glass windows
Filling space inside the capacious church
Sanctuary is different from that
Of two weeks ago as the sparkle of

The blues reds greens and golds of the glass is
Prominent and the pews and organ are
More visible and the candle light that's
Hanging on a chain from a wooden beam

And enclosed in a red glass container
Is no longer aglow in the darkness
But it still inspires a glow of warmth
Inside me as each of us is stepping

Quietly in line and meditating
With every step around the empty pews.

There is more light
in March but the air
is chilly and I look
forward to walking
barefoot in July.

After the Big Bang when the universe
Exploded from the size of a pinpoint
And thereby created the substance of
Space/time for millions of years clouds of gas

Radiated outwards that the force of
Gravity collapsed into the first stars
And for billions of years in the cores of
The most massive of stars where the pressure

Of gravity and temperature is
Highest nuclei of atoms were fused
Together forming new elements like
Oxygen and carbon and iron and

When the original stars convulsed and
Irrupted the cosmos was evolving.

The iron and carbon
in my body came from
a supernova billions
of years ago but how
did consciousness arise?

The laws of science can explain light and
Gravity and nuclear behavior
And by using radio-telescopes
Scientists can travel back in time and

Observe the radiation left over
From the Big Bang at the remotest edge
Of the cosmos in any direction
And they postulate that the universe

Is expanding — and they have fashioned their
Minds into marvelous instruments but
They have no explanation for how their
Consciousness came to be except to say

The random interaction of matter
Somehow produced their curiosity.

Perhaps the cosmos
is permeated
with consciousness and
the galaxies and the
atoms are its body.

A watery snow in April summons
The worst in me because I clear my own
And my mother's driveway too every time
The weather turns and in April I think

It shouldn't be snowing anymore and
It should be raining — if there is any
Disharmony within my acquaintance
It is sure to blossom in resentment

As I am moving snow — but I know my
Emotions are wayward and I practice
Letting them go and when I am finished
Writing this poem my mood will be light —

April snow is not the worst occurrence
And I am grateful I can change my mind.

Two hurricanes in
Puerto Rico
devastated the island
leaving everyone bereft
and sweltering in summer.

I am looking at a blue sky through a
Window sitting on a comfy office
Chair with arm rests warm and comfortable
In early April when there shouldn't be

Any snow on the ground after I raked
Snow from one roof and cleared two driveways and
Two walkways and one porch with my fingers
On the edge of freezing and now I am

Drinking coffee and the snow is piled as
High as it was months ago and is the
Quantity of light greater than it was
But the season is overwhelmed by an

Intrusion of arctic air or is the
Earth wobbling and bringing an ice age?

I dreamed of driving to
Baraboo Wisconsin in March
to converse with a
friend but this morning it seems
February has returned.

It is anomalous for April to
Be as frozen as February in
The morning and it seems that the jet stream
In the troposphere is flowing in a

Pattern and sweeping Minnesota with
Arctic snow and cold when in other years
We would be seeing tulips by now and
This morning while driving down a hill I

Saw several kids huddled in a group
Waiting for a school bus as a gust of
Wind raised some freshly fallen snow from a
Pile by the street and the snow swirled in

The air and I saw one little girl's long
Hair streaming in the wind for a moment.

I lose my morning
clarity moving
snow before it melts
and clogs the blower
in the afternoon.

There is a robin in the apple tree
And another has appeared and they are
Hopping about the tree and on the ground
And now they are gone and everything else

Outside my window doesn't look like spring
And I am grateful we didn't get the
Four to eight inches of snow forecasted
And we only have a frosting of snow

This morning but I am losing track of
Time and where did the months go while I was
Looking out this window looking forward
To spring and yet the same bare brown branches

Are stretching under a white sky and the
Sun is a white disk with a white halo.

My authority
the weather app on my phone
shows temperatures
in the forties and fifties
on Tuesday Wednesday and Thursday.

The nearest star to earth is four million
Light years away and yet there are billions
Of stars whirling around the massive black
Hole at the center of our galaxy —

The Milky Way — and our sun and earth and
Our neighboring planets are orbiting
Together in a spiral around the
Black hole at two hundred kilometers

Per second and yet it takes two hundred
Forty million years for us to orbit
The galaxy — and the galaxy as
A whole is careening at six hundred

Kilometers per second within a
Cluster of interwoven galaxies.

We are like clever ants
with glasses who are
scrutinizing and
conceptualizing
dark mass and energy.

I admire the romance of the stars
Leonardo Dicaprio and Kate
Wislet in the iconic scene of the
Movie *Titanic* at the prow of the

Ocean liner when they face the icy
Wind and ride the turbulence of the sea
And I would like to do the same but I
Don't know which direction to stand into the

Rotation of the earth on its axis —
And I would like to ride the turbulence
Of space as the earth is going about
The sun — and join the solar system

Sojourning around the galaxy — but then
Where on earth is the galaxy going?

Gripping the armrests
of a comfy chair I am
tumbling in four
directions at once without
a smidgeon of dizziness.

It is fun to play with the lingo but
When talking to a real scientist I
Get a little dizzy and I am not
Sure whether my question is bizarre and

Is he saying something intelligent
That seems to make sense or is he confused
And doesn't know the answer or is he
Passing on some knowledge and in effect

Is saying — you figure it out — because
I really want to know the direction
From where I am now to face into the
Rotation of the earth on its axis

But all he did was point to the sun and
Remark that is where to get my bearings.

I wonder whether
disorientation and
dizziness has a
relation to the wavy
wacky multiversity.

Today is the seventy-forth day of
February with snow in the forecast
For tomorrow and in two days also
With an intervening day of sun to

Imagine what spring would be like if it
Came and now I am resting after the
Snow blower sputtered and expired and I
Shoveled a foot of heavy snow with the

Snow sticking to the shovel and I knocked
The shovel on its side on the asphalt
To un-stick the snow from the metal and
Then I thrust and knocked and thrust and knocked and

Finally I am finagling like
Crazy to turn complaints into humor.

The earth revolves and
the sun is stationary
so when I see the rising
sun I am facing the
earth's rotation.

On this the seventy-fifth — and the first
Of its kind — day of February I
Established for myself a separate
Peace and because my snow blower is broke

I will do as the people of yore have
Done after another fall of snow and
I am determined now to tred upon
The snow and crush it and not remove it

By shovel or other mechanical
Contrivance and I shall not think about
The snow or be disturbed about the snow
But yea will I remember that the Lord

Gaveth and the Lord will taketh away
And the sun will shine and the day be good.

Nicolaus Copernicus
was the first to see
the sun is not rising
the earth is spinning
towards the morning sun.

There may be a heaping of snow on the
Ground in the second half of April and
The trees are frozen in time just as they
Were in December and the chill rising

From the piles of snow is penetrating
But the robins have returned and today
I saw a squadron of the tiniest
Ants trespassing on the kitchen floor — and

The sun is half way up in the morning
And is a glorious force coming through
The window — and crystals in the snow on
A bush a foot away from me through the

Glass are refracting the sunlight into
Pinpoint jewels of green blue red and yellow.

So many things are
transpiring at once
coming and going and
even my emotions
even out.

We haven't seen Karl for a long time and
We don't know when the meeting ends whether
We will see each other again but if
There's a history of attendance it's

Easy to assume we will meet again
Tomorrow — not everyone comes every
Morning but some of us come several
Times a week so we rely on a room

Full of drunks wanting sobriety and
Assuming a sense of mission who are
Working a program of recovery
And we are more light-hearted together

And we speak honestly among ourselves
Which is much better than drinking alone.

Over time some of
us return crestfallen
after a bout of
drinking to a welcome
but some of us disappear.

Even when April rain is replaced with
Snow there is radiance in the season
When a crust of leftover ice is on
The ground and a bitter wind is howling

Through the days and the sky is mostly grey
There is radiance as we celebrate
Karl who died of alcoholism and
Grief because his son died before him and

We are gathered in the sanctuary
In the middle of an April blizzard
Remembering Karl's buoyancy and his
Big hearted bantering and the light is

Mingling with the clouds and the snow and
Becoming radiant in the stained glass.

The radiance is
mixed with sorrow and
we shouldn't be hard
on ourselves for
questioning.

A solar wind radiates outwards from
Our sun far surpassing the planets of
Our solar system making a bubble
That scientists call a heliosphere

Where pushing out encounters pushing back
From interstellar space and because the
Sun rotates once every twenty-five days
There is a spiraling of magnetic

Wind particles flowing out to meet a
Continuously shifting boundary
Where the solar wind slows and stops — where the
Pressure of the interstellar wind is

Enough to create a balancing of
Whirlwinds permeating the universe.

In Minnesota
a jet stream of polar air
is turning spring rain
into winter blizzards and
all I can do is wait.

The sparrows in the apple tree are here
For an instant and are going while the
Air is moist and the sky is threatening
To snow — and I am frustrated waiting

For a friend to do what needs doing and
Am wondering if I could have managed
Better — and I would like to give as much
Weight to my frustration as I do to

The sparrows in the apple tree and I
Would like to pretend the gloomy day is
No more imposing than a summer cloud
But things are happening just as they are —

I will improvise and do what I can
And tomorrow will be another day.

Sparrows are flitting
an eagle is circling
a squirrel is hopping
in the soggy snow and
I am watching.

It may be below freezing now and cold
Enough to snow — and the two driveways I'm
In charge of may be half covered from the
Last falling of snow — because my blower

Broke and I was too disgusted with the
Snow trespassing too far into April
To make the effort to shovel the whole
Driveway — but the forecast temperature

For this afternoon and the next four days
Is above freezing and is for mostly
Clear skies and so I can savor the chill
Rising from the snow as the weakening

Embrace of winter and I will wash my
Polar fleeces and put away my boots.

All the bare branches
of these drab brown trees
will be sprouting buds
and then the leaves will
be sighing in the breeze.

Henry has kidney disease and there is
No cure but symptoms are treatable with
A syrupy concoction that I draw
Into a syringe in the morning and

The evening and he sees me coming
But I am quicker and I get behind
Him and pull his face back and quick like the
Devil the medicine squirts down his throat

That he doesn't like so much but soon gets
Over when I give him his food — I do
All this while groggy from waking up and
As the minutes go by I enjoy my

Alertness and when I clean the box I
Notice his urine is syrupy goo.

It is sticky
going in and sticky
coming out and
the cat box is
messy.

Kit lets me know when he wants more food by
Knocking a container off the kitchen
Counter onto the floor and then he looks
At me and yowls and I see he's got me

Trained as I could choose not to respond but
Usually he gets as much as he
Wants because he insists and I'd rather
Have quiet in the house — but every day

I notice there are new scabs about the
Top of his head and inside and outside
Of his ears and I wonder whether he
Itches all the time or he is nervous

And is compelled to punish himself by
Scratching furiously with his hind nails.

In the world of
cat psychology
do maladjustment
and phobia arise
with intelligence?

It is easy to do the same thing at
The usual time to balance chaos
And when I am spooning cat food into
Dishes and separating the three cats

So that they don't trespass on each other
I could be burning with frustration with
A person who is not present at the
Moment or when I am brushing each cat

And also singing to them I may be
Occupied with a little triumph of
Yesterday but if I am nimble in
The morning especially nimble I

May be able to simply spoon the cat
Food and then brush each of the cats in turn.

Instead of falling
into a funnel of
emotion I would
rather sing nonsense
to the cats.

Time is slow after forty minutes of
Meditation in the morning because
The sitting quietly is like leaving
The aperture of a camera open

Enough to accumulate light and more
Of the world enters my gaze — and it takes
A long time for a bird to cross from one
Tree to another — and I admit

How tricky it is to identify
The beneficial effects of doing
Zen — because I will never know how I
Would have behaved apart from doing Zen

But I believe I am more thoughtful which
Is something I could easily have missed.

Years of meditation
allows more of life
to accumulate.

It is not every day that the sky is
Open but when it is I can see the
Contrails of airplanes in the distance — and
The warmth descending today creating

Puddles everywhere is a welcome change
And the bush outside the window is free
Of snow and sparrows are hopping up the
Trunk of the cottonwood and little birds

Are flitting between the trees in the back
Yard and there isn't any wind and I
Watch everyday but rarely see that the
Atmosphere and sunlight make a blue sky

On a clear day with a white rim along
The far horizon and I don't know why.

Last week a dozen
eagles were circling
slowly not far up
and sparrows were
darting below them.

On a third day of a clear sky I am
Driving between Stillwater and Bayport
And there are the crumpled leaves from autumn
And the morning sun is drenching the grass

And the grass is beginning to green and
I see the bare branches of bushes and
Trees that at a distance look like smudges
But in passing their twiggy forms emerge

Into wild curves and crooks and every limb
And twig is reaching up and outward to
Capture rays of sun and I remember
How winter wind sounds in barren branches

And what a difference the leaves will make —
The difference of howling and sighing.

Even when I am
driving by and occupied
with politics the
trees communicate
messages.

The comprehensive effects of winter
Are easy to miss month after month as
I hunker down and limit myself but
With the lifting of the temperature

There is liberation and today I
Rummaged through a container of shoes and
Discovered shoes untouched and forgotten
For a dozen years and I am appalled at

Some of the judgments I made and am
Sorry for the money wasted but am
Also enthused to put on a spiffy
Style in spring because it's been depressing

To wear the boots spattered with the salt the
Road crews use to melt the ice on the roads.

Like a turtle
in a shell I
sheltered within
but spring summons
peacock flamboyance.

I was given the lens of seeing and
The ear of hearing coming along with
The responsibility of choosing
And creating a direction that suits

Me that no one else can duplicate — and
When I am ruminating and searching
For words I sometimes do touch a meaning
That is difficult to communicate

And it is important to cultivate
The conviction that the messages I
Am seeing hearing intuiting are
The messages I am meant to receive

Because I am an individual
Swimming in a sea of interaction.

Experience is
transforming
with every step —
outside in and
inside out.

Is there any escaping the tension
Between love and hate even if there is
Awareness that whatever I perceive
Is only a slice of a larger whole

And even if there is exhaustion with
Competition and belligerency
Is it possible by an exercise
Of will to extinguish the revulsion

But preserve that which captivates my heart
Because emotions arise within me
And sometimes I chose the arising and
Sometimes the arising chooses me and

Anyway my consciousness is consumed
With reverberating contradictions.

Teachers convey
compassion
benevolence
equanimity and
altruistic joy.

It is necessary to see anger
Is the problem and it doesn't matter
Whether it is justifiable and
Doesn't matter if it's motivating

Anger alters reality and is
Difficult to escape — and it fills a
Body with furious energy but
Afterwards there is deflation and self-

Pity — and anger radiating out
Invites recrimination coming back
Without remedy — but imagine joy
And happiness and liberation and

What could be more vital than evading
Cancerous inexhaustible anger?

The world is burning
from a point of view
but today the sun
is brilliant and the
sky is resplendent.

There is a cosmos beyond the blue sky
That humanity has been ignorant
Of until quite recently and we are
Lucky to have a single sun and a

Moon that balances the earth's wobble that
Provides us with reliable seasons
Because it's not uncommon for two or
Three suns to orbit each other making

Stability impossible for a
Planet and imagine being on a
Planet flung into interstellar space
By the wild oscillations of two suns

Because without a sun at just the right
Distance we would not have a shining sky.

The sun the moon and
sky are mysterious
and miraculous but
usually we are too
busy too notice.

Gravity collapses clouds of gas to
Create the stars of differing sizes
And many are more massive than our sun
But the mass of every one is crushing

Inward on a core where the pressure on
The nuclei of atoms overcomes
The resistance of positive charges
To fuse the protons together and an

Explosion of energy and heat and
Light pushes outward and establishes
An equilibrium of forces and
From the core of our sun it will take ten

Million years for a photon to reach the
Surface — and eight minutes to strike the earth.

Energy passes
through my optical lens and
through my synapses
to my visual cortex
and then I can see the clouds.

There are nights when I am lying in bed
And cannot turn off my thinking and thoughts
Go around and around signifying
Nothing but restlessness and there are nights

When I am a hero in epical
Fantasies and once I was flying in a
Stadium and everyone was watching
Me but it's necessary every day

To provide myself with a good night of
Sleep and even if I become wide-eyed
With fear in a phantasmagorical
Dream I need the separation from the

Normal tensions and frustrations of life
Because when I sleep well I am awake.

Sometimes I wake up
wrapped in the sheets like
an eggroll because
my body begat
centrifugal force.

There is no mitigation of the shame
And no deflection of the anger that
The drunk who drives and injures innocent
People incurs especially when he

Understands the next drink could trigger a
Loss of consciousness when in the act of
Walking and talking and drinking he no
Longer knows what he is doing — except

To say that the alcoholic can't stop —
And the condemnation of the world will
Not change the fact until he surrenders
And time in jail or in prison may be

Justified and helpful in creating
A moment of healing desperation.

Alcoholism
progresses like
Alzheimer's and the
personality
slowly goes.

Little green buds are dotting the trees of
Stillwater and the sun — half way up — is
A brilliant disk radiating warmth and
The green of the grass is assertive and

Unstoppable and days of snow and ice
Of snow falling from a white sky with an
Absent sun and penetrating cold with
Piles of snow lining the streets everywhere

Those days are impossible now and yet
I am weary from the lingering fact
Of winter and when I see a friend with
The clarity of spring there are wrinkles

Around his eyes I didn't see before
Lending a smile a little more meaning.

I saw a pair of
cardinals one after the
other frolic in
the bush outside the window
before they flew away.

It is a day I've been expecting for
Many days and I would have to be dead
Not to celebrate the awakening
Of spring because my body has endured

Another winter and I remember —
And there is a bizarre simplicity
That a disk of white fire rising in an
Empty sky could prompt the budding trees and

The growing grass — and the curving twigs of
The cottonwood are sporting sprays of seeds
That look like decorations and when I
Close my eyes my eyelids are red with light

And my face is bathed in warmth again and
I imagine myself a tomato.

A cardinal flies
from a lower to a
higher cottonwood branch
and the sun makes
its wings shine.

Once I got on an airplane and went to
The other side of the earth to find home
But when arriving I was a stranger
To myself and to the Japanese — who

Didn't ask me to come — I wanted an
Adventure and excitement and I learned
Excitement is the management of a
High level of fear — and for the nine years

Of living in Japan I encountered
Unpredictability and turning
Points and when returning to Stillwater
I discovered more unpredictable

Turning points and where ever I reside
There is something unexpected coming.

We are human animals
growing roots into the
stories we tell ourselves
in an effort to manage
unpredictability.

I am awash in waves this morning with
The windows of my car open with the
Warmth coming in and I am bombarded
With the vibrant blue and white of the sky

And I am absorbing an explosion
Of tiny green leaves on the browns of the
Trees and an exhibitionist in a
Purple shirt is walking with his dog and

There is a sprinkling of dandelions
Already and a red wing blackbird is
Flying and when I get to the office
To play with words a yellow and a red

Tulip by the garage are reminding
Me cresting waves of light are everywhere.

Waves of light rippling
in the air enveloping
me separating me
from winter are exactly
what I wanted.

We were talking about how to deal with
Alcoholics from a family point
Of view and the two older ladies who
I assume came together as comrades

Were listening attentively next to each
Other with upside down smiles and they were
Calm and serious and settled within
Themselves and it was apparent they were

Capable of separating nonsense
And propriety and while bringing a
Message of spirituality and
Hope I find humor is harmonious

With the mission and I thought I saw a
Twinkle in their eyes of acknowledgement.

While sharing a
message of recovery
there is resonance
with the words in the
slightest of gestures.

I left my phone charging all night again
And it was very hot when I unplugged
It — and the display was frozen with the
Icon saying — life is good — so I pushed

The button to no avail and took the
Battery out repeatedly which is
Supposed to re-jigger the phone when the
Battery is reinserted and I

Heard a click and saw a point of blue light
Flicker and then a display pronouncing
— Welcome — arose followed by the — life is
Good — revelation — again so I am

Holding the phone against my cheek thinking
I could have used this for warmth in winter.

Can't make a call
can't surf the Internet
no music at the gym
no driving directions no
email no weather info.

It is necessary after buying
A phone to enter a secret password
As a matter of privacy that must
Be entered repeatedly and mine is

Abracadabra1 that I am sure
No one will guess — but it's laborious
To type twice for each application and
My fingertip is blunt and the key is

Tiny and the letter becomes a dot
That can't be read and I fumble and don't
Know whether I typed correctly and I
Get blocked because my identity can

Not be verified repeatedly so
I fight the urge to step upon my phone.

There is a
labyrinthine world
of crypto-technology
of hackers and bots
but I just want music.

Society in America is
Evolving as the old industrial
Infrastructure is being replaced with
The technological innovation

Made possible by computers and the
Internet — and enthusiasts proclaim
Finally people will be free from the
Drudgery of labor but what will the

Truck driver do if he is replaced by
Self-driving vehicles and would it be
Enough to endlessly play video
Games and watch movies on Netflix and post

Messages on Facebook or wouldn't he
Rather find satisfaction by working?

How will people of
average ability
find satisfaction
by playing games
instead of working?

For a change we were meditating in
A cabin in the country and a fly
Was touching our ears with a whine in the
Air — or maybe we were touching the whine

With our ears — over here and over there —
And after our sitting we went outside
With a chainsaw and traffic and music
In the distance and birds nearby and a

River rippling and reflecting and
The clouds transforming and the toppled trees
And leaves decaying in the water and
Infinite detail is impossible

To describe — except that I am touching
And being touched differently than you are.

The compulsion
to be productive
lifted and
consciousness
liberates.

The cottonwood leaves are half-grown outside
My window today and I remember
All the previous years of seeing the
Leaves half-grown and shining in the sunlight

But now I know beyond the sky there are
A hundred billion stars in the Milky
Way and beyond that there are a hundred
Billion galaxies with a hundred

Billions stars in each galaxy and each
Galaxy is expanding rapidly
In the universe and with that context
The reliable seasons of earth seem

Like a separate cottonwood leaf in
The infinity of the cosmos.

Intelligence
curiosity
instability —
I need direction
to channel my energy.

To grasp the meaning of a large number
I need a method of recognition
To furrow my forehead and a million
Seconds amounts to eleven and one

Half days — and a billion seconds amounts
To thirty-one and three quarter years — and
A trillion seconds approaches about
Thirty-two thousand years — and light moves through

The vacuum of space faster than any
Thing at a rate of one hundred eighty-
Six thousand miles per second and the light
From the furthest edge of the universe

Takes about forty-seven billion years to reach
The earth — which is a lengthy afternoon.

A microsecond
is one millionth of one
second — a nanosecond
one billionth and a
picosecond one trillionth.

Imagine a smiling waiter bringing
You a dish of your favorite ice cream
Every second for a trillion seconds —
He will be approaching you while you are

Having coffee with your friends and he will
Be elbowing you while you are driving
To Stillwater and he will be stacking
Dishes while you are taking a shower

And you could not escape him if you were
Giving a speech at a symposium
And if you don't bequeath his services
To your closest relative when you die

He will appear at your resting place for
Thirty-one thousand nine-hundred odd years.

Or you could dispense
with the bother and
receive your allotment
of ice cream in a
trillion picoseconds.

Pointy headed scientists insist the
Universe originated from a
Space no larger than a trillionth of the
Period at the end of this sonnet

And they say in a picosecond the
Cosmos popped into existence in a
Big Bang and was approximately ten
Thousand trillion trillion degrees — which is

Pretty hot — and in a nanosecond
The mass equal to the mass of our own
Milky Way was packed in the space of a
Hydrogen atom — which is pretty dense —

And they say space did not exist until
Popping matter gave itself its texture.

It takes me more
than a nanosecond
to comprehend this
information — more even
than a microsecond.

It is deplorable that a straw was
Discovered in the Marianas Trench
And perhaps to rescue the earth from the
Dispersal of disposable items

It may be helpful where possible to
Turn our implements of convenience
Into fashion accessories and I
Imagine a boutique establishment

Selling remarkable straws with perhaps
Titanium for a military
Gentleman with a tortoise shell case or
Elongated simulated ivory

Or tastefully bejeweled silver or gold
For a status conscious mademoiselle.

We would favor the
planet and engage
ingenuity massage
egocentricity and
boost employment.

Under cherry blossoms on a splendid
Afternoon nothing could make the moment
Better as the blooms take away the strife
I carry and the delicacy of

The petals are captivating and I
Turn to the freshness of growing leaves in
Pioneer Park and the elevated
Bluff allows me to absorb the sweep of

The winding valley and the river and
The sun — in the distance there is the new
Crossing Bridge spanning the river at a
Great height with artistic lines — and the boats

On the water are miniscule but I
Discern a majestic paddle wheeler.

Bees are busy
in the cherry blooms
when weeks ago
the tree was frozen
the branches were bare.

The scent of apple blossoms and lilacs
And the reappearance of cherry blooms
After a prolonged and dreary winter
On the occasion of a sunny day

When the leaves are almost grown and the air
Is mild again are a resurrection
Of beauty and joy that remind me of
Light-hearted childhood and easy going

Faith that everything is OK — and there
Is a touch of sadness in knowing that the
Blossoms will scatter and the perfume will
Dissipate in a few hours but the

Sun will be prominent for many months
And we will have thunderstorms and lightning.

There is
nothing crabby
about luscious
crabapple
blossoms.

On the occasion of apple blossoms
I celebrate the flowering and the
Dissipation as the blooms delight me
With their delicacy and beauty as

They reappear when the leaves are almost
Fully grown and the sun is extending
Energy and the earth is reviving
And the grass is growing in a shower

Of light and the sky is brilliant again
And I wonder why I am moved by the
Brief blossoming of a flowering tree
Separate from the events of my life and

When the petals are dispersing onto
The asphalt of the driveway I am sad.

Why is the
appearance and
disappearance
so delicately
beautiful?

Women in cyberspace are out of touch
Which doesn't mean they have no influence
And I have dabbled on dating sites and
Fashioned a profile with photographs but

My enthusiasm is haphazard
Because there is a miniscule range of
Compatibility because I want
Someone luscious and lascivious and

They want someone with bags of money and
I am a wordy intellectual
Who is a visionary mystic — but
I am wearily insouciant too

And I can't summon the energy to
Pick up the phone and compose a message.

Somewhere
Cleopatra is
waiting but I
can't summon
intensity.

After waking I was sore below my
Belly and found a bulging red welt that
Wasn't there yesterday so I ransacked
My memory and remembered the strange

Sensation when lifting the one hundred
Pound dumbbell forty times in a row and
The unusual pain didn't slow me
But I am sphere of consciousness and

From the periphery events waylay
Me — and the doctor said that I ruptured
My abdominal wall by tearing a
A muscle and am rewarded with a

Hematoma that makes wearing pants and
Walking a delectable affliction.

He said I am
not young anymore
and it isn't a
hernia so really
I am lucky.

The river is rippling again and
The river is sparkling with light and
The river is also glassy and I
Am imagining the spinning of the

Earth and electro-magnetic waves and
Gravitational waves rippling in
The atmosphere and interstellar space
And I am absorbing waves of photons

And sub-atomic particles and am
Awash in micro and radio waves
And the earth is rolling about the sun
Compelled by sloping space and space is not
Empty but is undulating about

Me as if I were a prominent rock
Being polished by a musical creek.

Waves of light
are bouncing off the
white and purple lilacs
and cresting away
into my eyes.

I am ambulatory but mostly
Sitting because of the hematoma
Near my pelvis and when it burst in the
Night as I was tossing and sleeping I

Didn't notice until I gingerly
Pulled the elastic band of my shorts and
Saw the open wound and the smeared blood that
Stuck to hair and I ignored the tearing

Sensation because I am a tough guy
And I shaved around the area and
Cleaned the wound and applied a bandage that
Needed to be securely taped in place

And now I have to sit on my ass and
Wait because I can't be exercising.

I was a little
too enthusiastic
with a dumbbell and
won't do that particular
exercise again.

Atoms combine to form molecules and
There are as many molecules in my
Eye as stars in the Milky Way and the
Air I breathe and the water I drink are

The same molecules that living beings
Have breathed and drunk as long as beings have
Lived on the earth — and the hidden structure
Of the cosmos is identified by

The persistence of scientists while on
My own I operate in a narrow
Range of perception believing myself
The center of the universe — even

When I comprehend the fact that I am
A temporary sphere of consciousness.

Apple blossoms and
lilacs effuse a scent
wafting in waves of
molecules penetrating
me with happiness.

As I was lying in bed before dawn
There was the rain and the thunder through the
Window and I heard the curvature of
The earth rebounding in the thunder or

I thought so and then it was time to feed
The cats and change water in the water
Dishes and brush the cats and make coffee
And attend to the litter box and have

Breakfast and by the time the shaving and
Showering was done and I was sitting
Meditating on the zafu and the
Zabuton there was light and birdsong through

The window and I heard the various
Songs of the birds that words cannot capture.

It is easier to
to detach from disruptive
emotions when I
practice letting them go and
drink in the sights and the sounds.

I knew Clark as a red headed rascal
From New York City who was my roommate
In a half-way house and afterwards in
A rented house on Grand Avenue in

St. Paul when we were attempting to be
Free of alcohol and drug addiction
By going to meetings and practicing
A program more than thirty years ago

And his mother is a famous singer
Living a life of exclusionary
Celebrity and I knew Clark to be
Curious and adventurous and strict

With sobriety but he encountered
Some difficulty and ended his life.

At a gathering
of three thousand sober people
I was surprised to
be touched by memory as
his mother told their story.

Every addict trying to be sober
Has to surrender justifications
Because self-pity and resentments are
Poisonous and it is not helpful to

Dwell on unfairness when dwelling on the
Unfairness precludes optimism and
Strengthens the emotions of defeat — and
The balancing of thoughts and emotions

Goes on continuously in subtle
Degrees and if the addict neglects to
Communicate with fellow addicts and
Share in a strength of community that

Is founded on intangible power
He forgets that addiction is deadly.

Clark broke off
communication
and was lost inside
a labyrinth of
misery.

The monarch butterflies born in August
In North America will migrate the
Thousands of miles to California
Or Mexico and they leave in fall and

Return in spring and somehow may return
To the same tree — the three generations
Of monarchs that are born from the spring to
The end of July aren't hardy enough to

Fly the distance and they frolic in the
Air for only a few weeks before they
Die — but every monarch butterfly starts
As an egg becomes a caterpillar

Weaves a chrysalis about itself and
Epitomizes metamorphosis.

The fluttering
monarch butterfly
is delicately beautiful
and poisonously
unappetizing.

Maybe the monarch butterfly uses
The foothills of the Rocky Mountains as
A guide and in its course it traverses
Brooks and rapids and broad flowing rivers

And maybe on its journey it takes a
Break by the Colorado River
In the Grand Canyon — and afterwards it
Flickers up the cliffs and out again — and

When the wind blows and the rain is pelting
It would have to take shelter but it is
Hard to imagine such a delicate
Creature continuously fluttering

As if its motion and direction were
A destiny and a satisfaction.

The butterfly beats
the air with its wings
and by force of will
and leverage it stays
aloft and flying.

Just thinking about possibilities
Makes me excited because I could meet
Anyone on Facebook when I set up
A page and post an introductory

Message with the photo of me at the
Gym on the mat sitting in the lotus
Position as if I were doing Zen
While wearing my sleeveless exercise gear

Showing the Buddha and lotus tattoos
On my shoulders that will communicate
So much about me beyond what words can
Do and maybe I will become friends with

People in Germany and Katmandu
Or I could engage a celebrity.

Of course I could be
chatting with a vivacious
and dimpled blonde
who in reality is
an obese guy in Pittsburg.

It is a couple of vertical posts
And a couple of horizontal tops
That the Japanese call a tori gate
And they usually paint it vermillion —

The name tori means the abode of birds
And the gate has no purpose except to
Signify the crossing of the mundane
To the sacred and I like the simple

Symbol and wonder how many times a
Day I could exit the ordinary
And encounter the ethereal if
I were not in a rush to get things done —

Sometimes in a frenzy and sometimes in
A quiet moment I am bedazzled.

Little by little
or all at once
I see beauty
And vastness.

I can see the weight of a cottonwood
Puff floating in the air and the air that
I breathe is made visible when the puffs
Are floating — and the smaller ones will rise

And meander but the heaviest will
Drop consistently and I can follow the
Journey of one or I can consider
The multitude that reminds me of

The people on a congested street with
Each person on a mission while the whole
Is a spectacle of seeming chaos —
And then the puffs are caught up in a breeze

And the curving current is visible
In the sinuous flowing of the puffs.

The cottonwood leaves
are fully grown and
pristine — and the sun
is touching the green leaves
over layering yellow.

I am a child who desires the moon
Seeing its untouchable allure and
Watching its transformation from a sphere
To a crescent noticing its presence

Even in the morning and afternoon
Appearing in a blue sky surpassing
The clouds as a jewel always beyond my
Grasping as an otherworldly something

Though the moon doesn't have the drama of
A sunrise or the power to change the
Seasons and determine life and I know
It's just a rock without an atmosphere —

The moon is in my heart as a symbol
Of beauty outshining explanation.

The moon is just a
mirror of the sun
prominent in the
night and elusive
during the day.

Kit Cat wakes earlier than I do and
He is smarter than I prefer and he
Did something this morning for the first time —
He used the door to my bedroom as a

Drum to wake me up — and it sounded as
If he rose on his hind legs and hammered
On the door with all his weight with his front
Paws and he is weighty and sinuous —

And for a reason I don't understand
He wanted inside my room even though
There was an open window to look out
And listen out in the dining room — and

He just would not stop — and I thought if I
Surrender he will do this everyday.

Curiosity
and stupidity
got the better of
me — proving I am
a pushover.

Someday I would love to vacation in
The Bahamas or the Rocky Mountains
For an exotic experience but
Today I am at home in Stillwater —

And now spring is transitioning into
Summer without hindrance and all I have
To do is be attentive — and I am
Listening to the wind tossing the leaves

Throughout the morning the afternoon and
The evening and I am allowing
The persistence of the wind in the leaves
To fill me with unexplainable peace

And joy — and I don't need explanations —
The wind in the leaves is ethereal.

The trees tossing
in the wind are making
the breathe of life
audible and
visible.

The blue sky is exceptional and the
Earth appears blue from the vantage of the
Moon and there is not another planet
With breathable blue air in the cosmos

We are aware of and we are searching
The fourteen billion light years of space and
Set among the brilliance of stars planets
Are almost impossible to find so

Given the impersonal and immense
Nature of reality there is no
Reason why the sound of the wind in the
Leaves should be so reassuring but then

In spring with the reappearance of leaves
There is the resurrection of sighing.

In the wind
in the trees the
breath of life
is audible
is visible.

Rain drumming on the roof and flowing in
The metal downspouts with the cool moist air
Reminds me that this morning is forming
A new manifestation — as I am

Moving about the house feeding the cats
Emptying the dehumidifier
Washing the dishes while all the windows
Are open and I am wearing a warm

Shirt listening to the consistency
Of rain speculating — who will be there
This morning and what stories will there be —
And I like unpredictability

Balanced with a reliable routine
Forming this immaculate morning.

Rain drumming on
the car — going
to meet friends.

It is helpful to set aside some time
After feeding the cats in the morning
To cross my legs and straighten my back and
Circle my hands with the tips of my thumbs

Touching — and while my body is poised and
Relaxed my mind discloses itself to
Me and there may be conversation from
A phone call or music from yesterday

Or maybe an old pattern will assert
Itself rehearsing an aggravation
That may be mixed with satisfaction and
Sometimes I imagine thoughts arising

From the circle within my fingers as
The tips of my thumbs are barely touching.

I hold my thoughts
gently within my
fingers and palms
and my thumbs are
poised touching.

I need to be gentle with myself when
There are no easy solutions and my
Mind returns to comparisons and
Justifications and the unfairness

Of circumstances because I am not
The only person who feels gloomy on
Occasion — and I need to recognize
That sometimes my intellect becomes a

Labyrinth of contradicting puzzles
With my thoughts churning uselessly — because
That is what my thoughts and emotions do
Sometimes when I assume a point of view —

When I don't know what to do with myself
I have to believe I am loveable.

I am
exquisitely
situated to
discover what
love is.

Once a month I leave my Zen Bridge group of
Meditators after meditation
And do without the conversation at
The coffee shop and go to a meeting

Of Washington County Republicans
For conversation at a family
Owned restaurant and though the differences of
The groups are not as tribal as between

The Irish Catholics and the Protestants
I do approximate being a spy
In suspicious camps and touch the edges
Of the sharp attitudes on either side —

Sharing a mission and urgency is
Intoxicating — letting be is hard.

There is enough
deluded honesty
to keep everyone
enthusiastic
and arguing.

As a consumer of the news and a
Composer of essays I reinforce
My compendium of data points and
Marshall my facts in order but unlike

My colleagues I don't go to bed and wake
Up angry and I'm not surrounded by
Politicos and activists burning
With the latest outrage and if I were

Whom could I trust? Every morning my cats
Are awake before me and they express
Uniqueness without sophistication
And this morning there is a steady breeze

And the leaves are tossing and creating
The most peaceful and satisfying sound.

The simple fact
of breathing and
beginning the day with
optimism is
unsurpassable.

My chin is on the heel of my hand and
My elbow is placed upon a board that
Serves as a desktop for a keyboard and
A computer — and I am quite confused —

Because it seems the computer the board
And me — and the cottonwood outside the
Window — are each composed of atoms with
Nuclei around which electrons are

Swirling — and it seems that most of the space
That encloses atoms is empty and
So everything about me consists of
Essentially empty space and yet I

Recall the morning a pileated
Woodpecker was pecking the cottonwood.

Are the words that
arise from the
molecules
of my brain
empty?

Somehow scientists identify the
Nature of particles much too small to
See by using logical deduction
By employing precise instruments like

The Large Hadron Collider that is a
Twenty-seven kilometer ring of
Superconducting magnets that directs
Streams of particles accelerated as

Fast as possible into collision
Exposing gluons and bosons and quarks
And leaping leptons and matter anti-
Matter annihilation revealing

If God created the earth in seven
Days God is capable of precision.

Beyond our
technology
there is only
mathematical
postulation.

It's amazing a mathematician
Can compose an equation describing
The curving space of a hillside in terms
Of mass and energy — and amazing

Scientists also dissect the cosmos
Into relative speeds and distances —
And it is a little confounding that
An unrelenting application of

Logic and deduction exposes the
Terrifying impersonality
Of the immense and the minute without
Providing a basis for compassion

Or for a very useful description
Of being alive and learning to love.

Once I became
a father I don't
believe there's
ever an end to
being a Dad.

Walking underneath the rain I am more
Receptive than I know when a single
Drop impacts upon my forehead — but not
Until I saw the size of the spot of

Wetness on the concrete and I passed a
Puddle and noticed the splash and ripple
Was I fully aware these were very
Big raindrops falling from the clouds — and I

Recalled a moment ago the instant
Of being struck the size of the plop was
Apparent but I would not have noticed
Without the reinforcing evidence

Everywhere before me — proving I am
A vessel of transient sensations.

Rain is falling
in waves of
intensity and
they are slanting
in cool gusts of wind.

Dear reader if you are reading me now
You have probably read other poems
Also and I would like to thank you for
Your interest and your time and by the way

I am not gay but wordy and geeky
And like to figure things out and now you
Are the object of rumination — and
Because you are reading poetry and

Not obsessing on Facebook or Twitter
You are likely to be independent
And intelligent and I wouldn't guess
You're a man because men drive pickup trucks

And mess with tools in the garage so please
Know I am single and available.

You can always
reach me at
info@bumble.com.

Alligators and an impending sense
Of doom were the vestiges of a dream
That dissipated once Johnnie began
To incessantly yowl for his cat food

And I tried to remember the entire
Milieu of this episode of terror
But the details had slipped through my fingers
So to speak as I was opening the

Cans of food and separating the three
Cats into their isolated rooms and
All I could do was to ponder the world
Of physics and the scientist who wrote

The book I was reading last night who wants
Evidence of something deeper than quarks.

How can we
verify
measure
quantify
dreams?

It is there every morning in the tank
The surviving one of the four that lived
For twenty years and I remember my
Dad would drop the flakes of food and watch as

Silver dollars would flit so speedily
Around the water snatching the dropping
Flakes but my father died years ago and
I was not enthusiastic about

Maintaining the aquarium but I
Have a routine of changing the water
And cleaning the filter and feeding the
Fish and this one is more interesting —

He is about the size of a silver
Dollar with roving intelligent eyes.

He watches me
everyday and now
I am watching
him.

Jennifer is in my circle of friends
And she is the captain of a rolling
Rectangle that contains children on the
Way to and from a school and she enjoys

Driving the bus and she loves marshalling
The students and would like to continue
Everyday and Harold is a retired
Marine who also drives a school bus but

He comes to our circle with horrible
Tales of the devious behavior and
The disrespect he is attempting to
Endure — and maybe the assortment of

Kids is different or perhaps the
Permutations of the divers are key.

Over all there
could be a
balancing out of
repulsion and
attraction.

It's a dark morning with the watery
Sound of rain continuously coming
Through the windows and I have a choice of
Wearing long pants or shorts — and I'm not

Meeting anyone so there is no need
Of formality — and even though the air
Is chilly now it is most likely to
Be hot and muggy by this afternoon

So I will wear my shorts and my clogs too
Because I believe not wearing socks is
The epitome of liberation —
I was given the clogs and they are too

Big but I do like them — and now I will
Stay warm by wearing a long sleeve sweatshirt.

Sitting at my desk
I only have to
tilt my feet down
and suddenly
I am barefoot.

After the cats have been separated
And fed and then brushed they can do as they
Wish while I have to change the water in
Their dishes and attend to the litter

Boxes and the box upstairs is sticky
Because of the gooey medicine that
Henry needs for his kidney disease and
Then I can do as I want and coffee

Is a priority and this morning
While I read my daily meditation
Books on the periphery Kit Cat leaps
Through the air from the bed and he lands

With a thud on the floor and he thunders
After Johnnie into the dining room.

Henry likes to be
brushed and as I
sit on the floor he
nudges my calf with
the top of his head.

The solstice is approaching again with the
Counterbalancing of the longest day
And the shortest night and afterwards the
The nights will begin to lengthen until

A balancing with the shortest day in
December — while in Minnesota this
Morning it is chilly and damp and the
Ants are busy in a humongous hill

In my yard and the grass does need cutting
This afternoon and the temperature
Was ninety degrees a few days ago
But now a chill is returning in the

Morning — proving that we are never far
From February in Minnesota.

The border of my
yard along the street near
the corner of the
driveway shows the damage of
a reckless city snowplow.

Gravity and dark matter are drawing
The Andromeda and the Milky Way
Galaxies together and within four
Billion years the hundred billion stars of

The Milky Way will mix with the trillion
Stars of Andromeda as the black holes
At the centers of the galaxies will
Circulate and eventually will

Combine into one extraordinary
Black hole whirling all the stars in a new
Array and whether a passing star will
Strip the earth from our sun and into its

Orbit or fling us into empty space
Or whether we will be OK — who knows?

It is hard to tell
from my comfy office
chair that we are caught
in the spiraling of
the Milky Way.

We each have an individualized
Expiration date when our lives will end
And the earth is also not exempt from
A fiery death when the sun burns up

Its hydrogen and commences to fuse
Helium nuclei into carbon
And then the sun will swell hundreds of times
Bigger than now and the sun will swallow

The planets Mercury and Venus and
The sun will loom larger and larger and
The oceans will evaporate and the
Lands will be molten and there will be an

End of solstices equinoxes and
Lunar eclipses before the earth burns.

The sun will not be
a red giant in
an afternoon but
in five billion years
of afternoons.

From the vantage of today the Pueblo
People who lived in the hollows of the
Cliffs who built adobe homes and worshiped
The sun seem simple and innocent as

The sun was determinate of so much —
Drenching lifetimes with light — and imagine
The contrasting of the day with the night
With stars and the comfort of a small fire —

And perhaps they shared our frailties and
Were as prone to anger and fear as we
Are and they needed to ascribe meaning
To what happened by considering the

Constellations and by retelling the
Mythical stories about courage.

Even with our
knowledge of the
cosmos have we
outgrown needing
stories about courage?

A black hole that can whirl a trillion stars
About itself is not something that can
Be safely ignored and where do the stars
Go that disappear into the hole — and

It is said that vanished stars are compiled
On themselves to a point of infinite
Density inside the hole and said that
Millions of light years is not far enough

To escape the vortex of the hole and
It is speculated even space/time
Collapses inside the hole and time is
Instantaneous and so a word is

Used to describe the inconceivable —
The black hole is a singularity.

The hole where things
go to vanish is an
organizing factor
creating motion
and direction.

Imagine galaxies are vanishing
Beyond the horizon of telescopes —
Cosmic energy is dissipating —
The temperature is plummeting to

Absolute zero — the trillions of stars
Of the galaxies are flickering out —
The massive black hole of our galaxy
Is evaporating — imagine the

Dark mass and dark energy dissolving —
The universe is in a dark era
With molecules disintegrating — with
Particles diffusing and drifting and

At this curious time of day it would
Be difficult to make a ham sandwich.

I would be on the
corner checking the
weather app on my phone
waiting impatiently
for the next Big Bang.

Waiting and Loving

The attraction is understandable —
He speaks of hardship and aggression and
The advantages of retribution
That compelled the respect he exacted

And he told me that her mother believes
She is bad and never will be any
Good and that her ex-husband is using
Their daughter to sell heroin and that

Every member of her family would
Rather she remain an addict and a
Drunk but that she is doing her best to
Be sober and there is something about

Her that he loves beyond sympathy and
She is the only woman he wants.

There comes a wounding
that makes living differently
imperative and
he needs inexhaustible
power greater than himself.

It is nonsense to be asked to do a
Moral inventory on yourself when
You love an alcoholic and cannot
Stop loving her when she encourages

You and makes a show of caring about
You and sets the table for an evening
Of enjoyment but she disappoints and
Even seems to be purposely hurtful

And you are angry and confused and yet
Cannot stop loving her no matter what —
Sometimes doing what is necessary
Doesn't make sense within the chaos of

Alcoholism when everything you do
For her doesn't make any difference.

Didn't cause it
can't control it
and cannot cure it —
so why are you doing
what you are doing?

I admire a love hardy enough to
Endure the neglect coincident with
Addiction as the addict is rising
From deep waters and is struggling and

Needs to break to the surface and breathe the
Life giving air — and the addict is not
Capable of keeping promises or
Of making trustworthy choices or of

The giving and taking of love — because
Learning to love is difficult without
Experience — and I admire the
Willingness to wait for sobriety

But there is no guarantee that she can
Rise to the surface and emerge safely.

He loves the flair she
has in choosing clothes and when
they talk the night goes
by in an instant and
songs remind him of her.

The attraction is understandable
Because his mother practiced punishing
Him without motherly love and he learned
To harden his emotions as a child

And how is loved learned without a mother's
Original love? The woman he loves shared
The same privations and neglect and
They share the same suspicious attitude

And they did not escape the company
Of predators for many years but he
Sees specialness in her elevating
Her above the other women he knew

And this feeling of love arose and he
Was unprepared and disoriented.

He discovered love
makes the waiting
possible even
without a surety
of return.

He inherited from his mother a
Determination to seize what he wants
And he used his intelligence to see
The vulnerabilities in people

And he learned to apply leverage to
Bend people to his will and he was
Good at persuasion and he was better
At intimidation because he knew

Recklessness is terrifying but he
Also knows that fighting for the scraps he
Thought he needed among people who were
Just like him — even if he were stronger —

Brought him no satisfaction and there is
A hole in his soul he cannot ignore.

He knows he didn't
know how to live and
inescapable
meanness is
dispiriting.

He has absorbed the impact of car and
Motorcycle accidents and he feels
The left-over pain today and he was
As reckless as any addict could be

But he is not alcoholic and can
Stop drinking and drugging when he wants to
But living without satisfaction and
Loving a woman who is an addict

Brought the gift of desperation and drove
Him into the rooms of recovery
Because there was nowhere else to go and
He was willing to do anything to

Alleviate the perplexity and
The frustration and the futility.

When he held her hand
the connection was
different from any
other woman and she
sang and read to him.

She was not ready for marriage she said
And he waited a year and within the
Year she relapsed and in the summer there
Was rejoicing and in the autumn there

Was hesitation and he is waiting
Another year without conversation
With her but the songs he hears in stores and
The words he reads in books remind him of

Her and in the meantime he is learning
How to be respectful and kind with the
People he knows and he is opening
His heart for spiritual solutions and

He is abiding time with patience and
Growing roots into his higher power.

He's taking time to
listen to friends and to help
his father repair
a truck and renovate the
property and land for sale.

They call the building they converted from
A cattle shelter a shop and that is
Where he is in his free time with his Dad
Amongst mechanical equipment and

His Dad is divorcing a second wife
And Dad is a retired overland truck
Driver and Dad remains as stubborn as
Ever but is weaker and when working

With machinery Dad is easily
Confused and needs the knowledge and the skills
Of the son who can do in minutes what
Would have taken hours or would not have been

Done and if the son were not cooking the
Father would not be eating much at all.

When the son was young
the father thought it right that
the son struggle without
help because that is
what grandfather did.

His Dad is selling the house and the farm
And has been talking about going south
Away from the cold winters but Dad has
No definite place to go and Dad is

Always finding new repairs for the truck
And there's a futility about the
Talk as if Dad outlived expectations
And doesn't want to look beyond the next

Modification of the truck and the
Endless fiddling with mechanical
Things is all Dad can do and the son is
Taking the responsibility and

Seeing that Dad is eating and doing
What he can to make Dad comfortable.

The son talks about
moving to Colorado
but the question of
what to do with the woman
he loves is unresolved.

The mariners used sails to catch the wind
And sometimes they suffered under the sun
When there was no wind to move them — and God
Divided the Red Sea and rescued the

People from Pharaoh and He gave Moses
The Ten Commandments and the burden of
Leading the people in the desert for
Forty years — and the mariners didn't

Abandon the seas because they suffered —
And Moses didn't lead his people back
To Egypt because it was difficult —
Burdens are made lighter by sharing them

But the burden is heavy for leaders
Who find their courage when necessary.

Faith means doing the
best possible with
confusion and believing
something good
will happen.

Once there is a touch
of transformation
the mean old ways are
no longer appealing and
we wait for good direction.

— *Tekkan*

Everyday Mind VIII

The sky was clear but
now there is a
downpour and a
splashing of puddles
on my driveway.

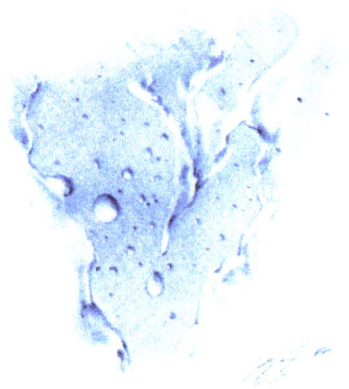

With the whoosh of the burner firing
I look up and see a hot air balloon
Floating in the air and it looks so odd
Suspended in the sky and there is the

Burst of flame and the rise of the balloon
And the gradual drifting and there are
The several balloons peopling the
Sky but the people are too far to see —

Only on the cloudless days of summer
Do balloons appear in such festive colors
And I imagine the buoyancy and
The view of the river on a sunny

Afternoon and there is no purpose for
The ride except for the effervescence.

What does the
valley look like with the sun
sparkling on the river
and reflecting off the windows
of the moving cars?

It is a human predicament that
We can't really live without relying
On some opinion about the after-
Life and the determination each of

Us makes is as much emotional as
Intellectual — and it's easier
To adopt a tradition and follow
A well-worn path — but I can't help thinking

One life cycle isn't enough because
Circumstances are limiting and I
Have my responses and outcomes that
Are only a morsel of what is

Possible — could I already be on
A journey of consecutive lifetimes?

The taste of life
is often bitter and
I seem compelled
to find a better
way to live.

The cottonwood outside my window is
Doomed because of a lightning strike from years
Ago that left a gash in the bark and
Exposed the core of the tree — and the tree

Has been leafing and filling the air with
Puffs as it should every year — and the view
From the window that inspires me in
The morning will never be the same — when

There was a white sky and snow on the ground
A pileated woodpecker appeared
And began to peck on the core of the
Cottonwood and I was enamored with

Its enormous size and with its crested
Red head but it was damaging the tree.

The arborist looked
at the exposed core and the
gaping holes and thought
such a gargantuan and
damaged tree was dangerous.

The cottonwood is doomed because of our
Decision to take it down before it falls
In a storm and damages the house and
The view from my window will be changed

Permanently which makes a difference
To me — for four years now every morning
I have come to my desk and window to
Capture something worth remembering and

Sometimes an event from yesterday comes
To mind but often when I am quiet
The most ordinary things emerge
In an extraordinary light and for

Years I have played with sunrises and light
And squirrels and birds and this cottonwood.

Through grade school
junior high school and
high school I didn't
notice this cottonwood tree
until I wrote poetry.

Each leaf of the cottonwood is taking
The sunlight and converting it to life
And energy and the tree is doing
Its part in effusing oxygen and

Thereby providing breathable air to
So many living beings but the tree
Experiences life differently
From me becoming responsive in spring

And frozen during the winter while I
Can marvel as the leaves are turning and
Sparkling in the light and I also
Appreciate its magnificence and

When the men with equipment come to take
It down that will be a very sad day.

The cottonwood was
present during my childhood
and when I returned
from living in
England and Japan.

My home is two blocks from my office and
My office is in the house where I grew
Up as I run the family business
That my Dad began fifty years ago

And it's remarkable that there are two
Towering cottonwoods in my life — one
Outside my window where I begin my
Morning by writing poetry and the

Other is on the corner of Martha
And Sycamore streets where my home is and
I have had to dispose of cottonwood
Leaves for over twenty years in the fall —

And I wonder how much different my
Life would be out from under cottonwoods.

When the wind is
moving cottonwood leaves
the breath of life
is audible
and visible.

I've worn glasses from my earliest years
And I am so used to seeing the world
Through gold rims and lenses that I never
Notice them anymore — and as I am

Sitting and standing and walking about
And lying down my arms and legs and hands
And feet are always visible but they
Are not the focus of my attention —

My body is a puppet and I am
The master pulling strings and behaving
As I please by showering dressing and
Eating — and I can get in a car and

Drive to a gathering of my friends and
Watch the other puppet masters playing.

A persisting
tooth ache is an
awakening — the pain
won't go unless I visit
a dentist.

The ownership of the hotel has changed
And all the managers who were there when
She started have moved on to better jobs
As this is chain of modestly priced

Hotels that doesn't pay employees well
But does fill with guests on the weekend — and
She has been named best employee of the
Month several times because she cleans each of

The rooms diligently and is cheerful
With the guests even when they are rude — and
Now every person who worked there when she
Began has left and she is loyal to

The guests and once in a while someone will
Recognize her worthiness with a tip.

She works
diligently
where others
just don't care.

The maintenance guy has quit — so there is
No one to fix the leaky faucet — and
The general manager used all the
Maternity leave she was entitled to

And then she quit — the typical sort of
Housekeepers can't be relied on to change
The bed sheets or scrub the toilets and they
Can't be depended on to show up for

Work — The hotel is down to a couple
Of front desk managers who do double
Shifts without assurance of relief — and
There are only several hardworking

Housekeepers cleaning and serving breakfast
And wondering — how long can this go on?

The hotel is booked
six months ahead and
looks like any other
establishment but the
management collapsed.

On a morning in July there are a
Few cottonwood puffs floating and there
Are two white insets flying sinuously
In a gloriously blue sky and they are

Chasing each other — and then I lose sight
Of them among the cottonwood leaves that
Are bright with sunlight — and the sun is an
Imposing white disk with a yellow fringe —

And I am happy to have attended
A meeting where we promulgated the
Importance of living in today and
Not yesterday or tomorrow because

We are never far from February
And shoveling snow in Minnesota.

As one among
sober alcoholics
it's good to
counteract
curmudgeoncy.

The deep grooves of the cottonwood bark are
Perfect for squirrels to clamber up — if
I were a squirrel the immensity
Of the cottonwood outside my window

Would be worth the exploration of a
Lifetime as there are pathways upwards to
A dizzy height that would be the end of
The world to a squirrel — and there is the

Temptation of the outward branches that
At the furthest extent dangle downwards
Challenging the courage of squirrels who
Have no reason to go there — I admire

The tenacity of compulsively
Climbing squirrels — don't they get exhausted?

Watching squirrels is
amusing and often
I don't really want
to turn my attention
to politics.

I don't know how to practice politics
And to associate with like-minded
Compatriots without also having
The suspicions and the bitterness that

We direct at people of opposing
Loyalties — because it seems that every
Organized political movement needs
Heroes and ideals that are worthy

Of sacrifice — and a party needs its
Oppressors and outrages against whom
Action is necessary — the drive for
Conquest makes a virtue of deception

And it takes honesty and compassion
To have opponents but not enemies.

History
is heroic
demonizing
romantic and
intoxicating.

I didn't feel the heat of the morning
Until the little black fly with green eyes
Landed on my arm and walked about with
Little legs over the fine hair on my

Arm — and I discovered not wanting to
Expend the energy necessary
To flick it away so I just watched it
Instead and noticed the slightest tickle —

And a little while later a tiny
Black ant proceeded to explore my arm
Too and I noticed the tickle again —
And the ants and the flies have as much right

As I do to enjoy the summer air
But I won't give the mosquitoes a pass.

As the air becomes
hotter even in the shade
of a tree I start
to feel a little dizzy
and warmer inside and out.

Kit Cat is drawn to the windows of our
Home and we have determined that he and
Johnnie and Henry are house cats to be
Fed regularly and freed from hunting

And killing — and it is a little sad
To hear Kit Cat whining at the window
And see him sniffing a summer breeze with
His ears forward and with his eyes focused

On something outside — and he is hunched and
Poised as if to pounce — but of course he can't —
And on the occasions when I step out
Without being careful and he escapes

He runs and hops — and he rolls in the dirt
And chews the grass — and he lets me catch him.

Kit is delicate
maneuvering among the
cans and packages
on the kitchen counter — front
paws precise — back following.

There are afternoons when I leave all of
The car windows open to feel the breeze
Blowing through and other days when it is
Better to use the air conditioner

When there is a moist and sticky feeling
About the heat — and in the middle of
July wind continues to toss the limbs
And leaves of the trees but the motion and

The sound aren't as noticeable to
Me as the heat and the sun are much more
Prominent but when I see the long leaves
Of a willow flowing within a breeze

All the elements I love about the
Summer are included with the willow.

There is fluid grace
about the long willow leaves
in a summer breeze
as the sun the wind and the
willow are in harmony.

I am now over sixty years old but
That has very little to do with my
Behavior because I go to the gym
And am especially spry and put the

Younger guys to shame in comparison
But it's been pointed out to me when I
Bend over to tie my shoe or when I
Rise from my chair at the coffee shop a

Groan will often escape from me — but I
Am not complaining because I wouldn't
Know I was doing it if the people
Nearby weren't informing me — anyway

I do remember long ago others
Letting me know that I was grimacing.

I am not in charge
of what my body does —
beyond the choosing
of the activity and
the energy expended.

I was walking with a friend who enjoys
Gardening and asked about a shrubby
Plant with tiny purple blossoms that we
Were passing by — because I was seeing

The plant everywhere while driving about
Stillwater and it was just another
Thing I didn't know — like the names of the
Different kinds of wildflowers — and she

Said it is a Russian Sage and that it
Blooms in July and August — and it's not
Important — like following the daily
News is — as it is just a happening

So easy to overlook — but now I
Am wondering does it come from Russia?

At the coffee shop
we discovered from the
Internet that it
is eatable and it is
useful for relieving pain.

It was Saturday afternoon with a
Week of bother behind me — and I was
Done with most of my chores for the day and
Didn't want to do anything extra

And because I had no plans and it would
Have taken effort to reach someone who
Probably would already be busy
By then I decided to take a nap —

Because the sunny linen on my bed
Was inviting — and I stretched out in a
Separation from consciousness — and when
I awoke the bottom of my left foot

Was cozy and I became aware of
Something furry — Kit Cat was joining me.

The nap was a
hole in a sunny
afternoon — and
then I went shopping
for groceries.

On Twitter people are allowed to type
Two hundred eighty letters including
Punctuation in the composition
Of a message that they can transmit on

The Internet — and there are millions of
People communicating messages
And a celebrity will acquire
Millions of followers who happily

Have access to a famous person's thoughts —
But the medium devolved into a
Method for exchanging insults and for
Empowering groups of enraged people

Who enforce politically correct speech
By attacking in a virtual mob.

People have taken
an empty form capable
of concise beauty
but they are cultivating
hostility.

Meeting a friend for conversation in
Downtown Stillwater and sitting on a
Bench by the river before the town is
Open for business in the morning is

The epitome of luxury as
The air is chilly but warming — and the
Sun is reflecting off the water in
Flecks of gold — and in the distance there is

The high span of the St. Croix Crossing Bridge
Stretching across the valley in graceful
Lines — and there are the several ornate
Riverboats with paddlewheels that are docked

Nearby — and we have the freedom to say
Anything curious or trivial.

An open sky is
reflective of boundless
possibility —
conversation often
prompts discovery.

I am not the center of anyone's
Attention except of my own and a
Hobby — like connecting isolated
Words — is helpful for lifting my center

Of gravity — because I know thinking
About disrespect or discourtesy
Or a lack of appreciation makes
Thinking in a lighter mood just about

Impossible — if I am relying
On a divine something at work in the
Way things are then I need to cultivate
The faith that the divine is not apart

From the problem I can not evade but
The divine is a part of the problem.

I can't solve all my
problems by playing
with words but by
playing with words
I am happier.

I may be unsophisticated and
Unfamiliar with the conceptions of
Scientific classification but
If there are three dimensions — up and down —

Left and right — forward and backward — along
With a fourth dimension of time why can't
We consider life that somehow emerged
From the material of particles

And molecules as a fifth dimension
And why can't we assign consciousness that
Supersedes the purposeful functioning of
A heart arteries and capillaries

As a sixth dimension including a
Spectrum of rhinoceros and human?

A spirit moves
choosing direction
and velocity
surrounded by
other spirits.

By the time Friday afternoon comes most
Of the oomph of the workweek escapes me
And the dissipation of energy
And focus is not intentional but

Is just a matter of habit — and on
Saturday morning I can wake an hour
Later and be liberated from the
Pressure of earning money — and the day

Has a touch of a holiday about
It that often extends into Sunday
Morning and afternoon — but once the dishes
On Sunday evening are washed an air

Of seriousness settles upon me
As I think about what I need to do.

As a conscious
tomato I would know
the sun and night
the heat and chill
and bug feet.

There is a video on Facebook of a
Couple of kids after a down pouring
Of rain who have goggles for swimming and
And a bicycle and some muddy ground

And one of them gets on the bike and grips
The brakes and the other kneels behind the
Back tire and while wearing the goggles with
Much joyful expectation he says "go"

And he is covered by a spattering
Of mud — which is an improvement of the
Jackson Pollack style — because Jackson was
Dripping paint on canvas by himself and

Jackson never did escape depression
But the boys together were jubilant.

Eventually
sophistication
spoils
spontaneity.

Stillwater doesn't have the Zen Temples
Kyoto has and doesn't have the Shinto
Shrines and the imperial palaces
Or the stone lanterns and tori gates

And in Stillwater we don't hear bamboo
Knocking together in a breeze and we
Don't have the rising and fading throb of
Cicadas that permeates the summer

But there is a majestic river in
Stillwater wider than the Kamo in
Kyoto and there are the limestone bluffs and
The historic courthouse with a cannon

And in summer there are humming birds and
Swallows and many kinds of wildflowers.

There is a mountain
in Kyoto where monkeys
live but in Stillwater
there are butterflies
and dragonflies.

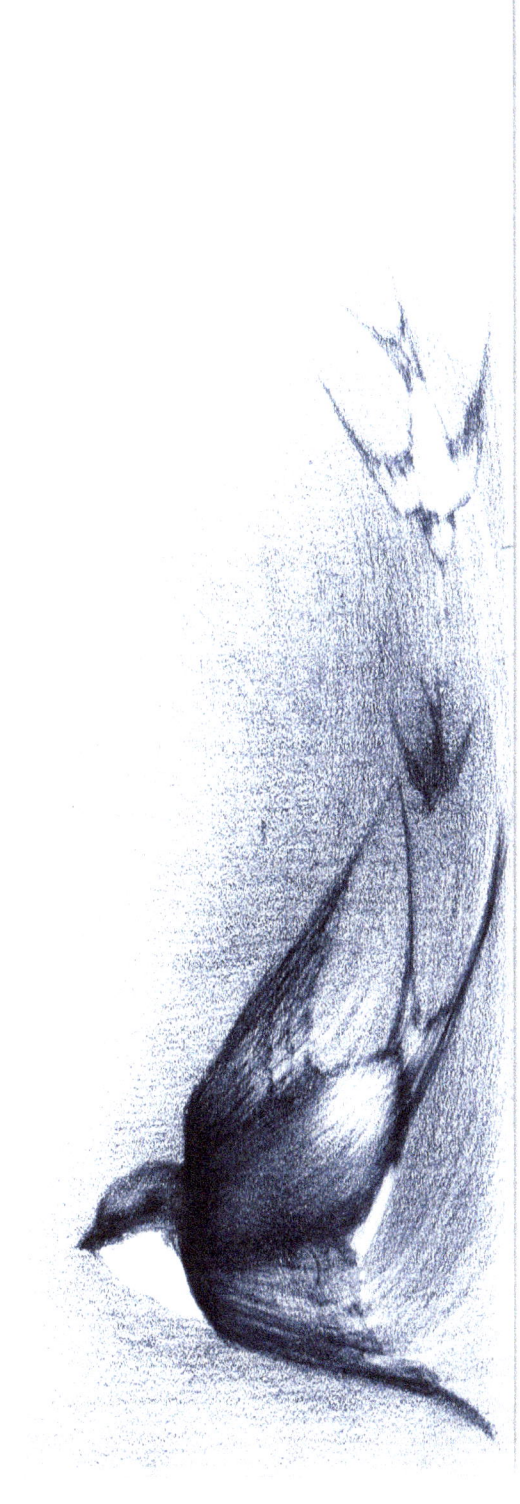

Kyoto and has a golden temple in the
North and a silver temple in the east
And there is a Zen rock garden where the
Monks rake the tiny pebbles sashaying

A harmonious pattern — and if you
See the traditional tile roofs of the
Temples and the homes you will not forget
The stylized mixture of pine trees and

Tiles — but there are also buildings made
Of concrete slabs that are stained by sticky
Smog along side the garish neon of
Pachinko Parlors where the Japanese

Play pinball while chain-smoking cigarettes
And staring with zombie fascination.

On television
Americans relive
cowboy shootouts and
Japanese cavort with
samurai slashings.

I embody and cherish the months when
I left my guest home in Yamashina
In the morning and walked over a ridge
Of mountains on the east side of Kyoto

For my destination downtown where I
Taught English in a language school and on
The way I passed bamboo and pine and the
Pagoda of the Kyomizu Temple

And the vermillion Ya Saka Shrine and
The Geisha district and the Kabuki
Theater — and I remember throbbing
Cicadas and the summer haze and the

Worn and secluded footpath and the view
Of Kyoto surrounded by the mountains.

I am following
Japanese masters
on their footpaths
collecting insights
for poetry.

I love peaches and am big fan of
The fuzz on the red and yellow skin and
When eating only a peach I close my
Eyes and think "I really do love peaches"

And usually it's my habit to
Slice a peach into sections and sometimes
I prefer thick slices and sometimes thin
But every morning is good with peaches

And blueberries and granola and milk
And my tongue will taste the blueberry and
My teeth will crunch the granola and the
Milk provides the slushy harmony that

Fills my mouth with goodness but it is the
Piquancy of the peach that is joyful.

I close my eyes
and can't stop
dreaming of peaches.

Blood Moon

In North America we weren't able
To see the lunar eclipse in July
That was the longest eclipse of the moon
By the earth in this century — but the

People in Africa the Middle East
And in Asia could have seen it if they
Had the inclination to watch sunlight
Passing through the atmosphere of the earth

And bending around the earth to fall on
The moon — and the watchers who know the facts
Would understand the air of the earth was
Scattering the shorter waves of blue and

Green and letting the longer waves at the
Redder end of the spectrum continue.

We comprehend so
many more facts about the
way things are without
satisfying the push
of our curiosity.

As it happens the astronauts who walked
About the moon came back with hay fever
With watery eyes and sore throats and the
Dust was clinging to their suits and clogging

Equipment and filling the craft with the
Smell of burnt gunpowder — the particles
Were fifty times as small as the width of
A human hair — and they are as sharp as

Glass — and because gravity is so much
Weaker on the moon when the astronauts
Moved in their land rovers they raised a cloud
Of dust that lingered around and because

There is no atmosphere the dust of the
Moon is electro-statically charged.

Fanciful stories
about the moon being made
of green cheese turn out
to be imaginative
nonsensical palaver.

When listening to the scientists their
Knowledge and their desire to conquer
Ignorance is obvious — and I have
The impression their wonderment about

The facts of the universe is burdened
With the fearsome immensity and the
Hostility to life that the cosmos
Reveals — moon dust is inhospitable

To breathing lungs — and some scientists do
Ascribe randomness to the way things are
That drains away any meaning any
Person would like to find in the events

Of life — to which I answer that life and
Consciousness are undeniable facts.

We cannot capture
and pin the butterfly of
divinity to
a board where everyone can
grasp its entire meaning.

Usually the alarm wakes me from
A dream and I am groggy — and my first
Sensation is the yowling of Johnnie
For his cat food — and I charge my cell phone

And tablet and make the bed and change my
Clothes and puff on the inhaler — that makes
Me rinse my mouth — and I squirt medicine
Inside of Henry the cat to treat his

Kidney disease and sometimes I may be
Distracted by an email while Johnnie
Is getting noisier and is yowling
Insistently because he is hungry

And wants his food while I appear to be
Quite unresponsive and indifferent.

On some days it takes
more time to get to Johnnie
and I must appear
a cruel and a capricious
kind of deity to him.

When I know what to look for I see it —
Almost as if the thing I was looking
For was waiting for me — but there is a
Side effect of having expectations

That by narrowing my focus I see
Less than I could otherwise — and I was
Driving around Stillwater on the third
Of August and there was a red leaf at

The top of a tree where I saw a red
Leaf last year that was a hint of autumn
Coming — and even though summer seems like
An established fact and winter seems an

Impossibility the sight of a
Scarlet leaf reminds me of transitions.

I also saw a
little yellow butterfly
flitting in a breeze
in its peculiar fashion
living a butterfly life.

I saw Kit Cat lounging on the window
Sill of my bedroom and he was absorbed
With the outside while I was making my
Way to the car to drive away and then

Quick like the devil he followed me out
The door and cavorted — and yesterday
After I gave him a dish of food that
Usually consumes his attention

I opened the door and reached for the mail
In the box and out scooted Kit Cat in
A snap — and then he cavorted — so I
Realize alertness is paramount

Because he may seem to be busy but
He is always conniving to escape.

His brain is the
size of a golf ball
and yet he is
making a monkey
of me.

We meditate in a little chapel
Inside a church for twenty minutes and
The Doan rings the bell and we stand up
And file out of the room on the way to

The sanctuary where we walk in steps
Of silent meditation for fifteen
Minutes — and we return to the chapel

For sitting meditation — the Doan
Stands by the door as we file in — and this
Morning after the first sitting I was
The last in line and I snatched the bell and

Carried it and on reentering the
Chapel I returned it to the Doan.

The confusion
and astonishment
in the middle of
the quiet was quite
satisfying.

We were putting the chapel in order
After we finished meditating by
Stacking the mats and cushions and
By returning the chairs to their places

Inside the chapel — after taking them
Out beforehand — and we were enjoying
Conversation in the vestibule as
We always do — and I was partaking

Of the meditative afterglow and
The clarity and reached in my pocket
For my keys — but they were not there — and I
Felt in my other pocket with no luck

Did I leave my keys in the ignition?
And did I lock myself out of the car?

I rushed on the
sidewalk expected the
worst but I noticed
the car keys were hidden
in my hand.

It's been discovered that the vacuum of
Space is not empty even though nothing
Is there — because in quantum space packets
Of energy are winking in and out

Of time — and no one knows where these tiny
Particles are coming from — and so the
Void of the cosmos is permeated
With an enormous quantity of what

Is believed virtual energy — and
I am wondering whether the thoughts I
Will have this afternoon that I have no
Conception of now will come from the same

Mysterious nowhere that the quanta
Come from — from a virtual consciousness.

Once in a while I
would appreciate
variety so
I could overcome the
drag of my habits.

The eye of science is relentless and
Scientists have found waves of gravity
And are postulating a gravity
Particle and they have discovered a

Particle that provides elements with
Mass they call the Higgs Boson that comes from
The Higgs Field — so I speculate — are they
Looking for the particle imparting

Consciousness — and if not why not — because
Consciousness is a reality and
We should have explanations to oppose
The randomality that drains meaning

From existence — because it would be good
To discover meaning in the cosmos.

If someday a
consciousness particle
is discovered I'd
suggest a name —
the Barry particle.

I imagine myself a simpleton
Moving about but only aware of
Two dimensions — forwards and backwards — and
Side to side — and if a sphere were imposed

About me — not being aware of up
And down — I could not incorporate the
Reality of the sphere extending
Above and below me — but I am not

A simpleton and I can understand
The third dimension of height and the fourth
Dimension of time and I can read what
Scientists write and can admire how

Far they are extending the boundaries
To what we can possibly understand.

Perhaps
a black hole is
an event involving
nine or eleven
dimensions?

A crew of five arrived in the morning
And they positioned a lift behind the
House near the cottonwood — and a man in
The lift cuts the tree with a chain saw — and

They placed a truck with a crane in front of
The house — and the guy in the lift attaches
The branches he cuts into cords the crane
Uses to raise the branches over the

House and onto the driveway — where the crew
Saws the branches into sections that the
Crane lifts into the trucks that will haul the
Cottonwood away — and I am watching

Through the window as the majestic trunk
Is standing but only for a moment.

Sawdust is
descending and an
open sky is replacing
a presence I've known
from childhood.

The cottonwood presented more heft than
The crew anticipated so a good
Length of the trunk remains this morning with
The familiar fork extending into

The sky and there is the clefting of the
Bark the two lightning strikes made and the holes
The woodpeckers left — and the largest hole
Was one of the reasons we decided

To take the tree down — but the branches and
The leaves are gone and I am facing the
Glare of the sun for the first morning with
An altered sense of normalcy and an

Appreciation for the heat of the
Sun that was filtered by cottonwood leaves.

In a week the crew
will return to take
the remaining trunk
with a machine to
grind up the stump.

The window serves as an extension of
My morning vision when I sit at my
Desk and formulate my thoughts about what
Is worthy of remembering today

And after surfing the Internet the
More than sixty people who were shot in
Chicago on the weekend and the blind
Eye the news media is turning to

The continuing catastrophe of
Violence and mismanagement of our
Largest cities demands attention but
The politicians and commentators

Would much rather talk about palaver
Personality and peccadilloes.

Everyday I looked
past the cottonwood seeing
neglect and bitterness
and I'm trying to be
optimistic.

There is a greyhound in this poem that
Is beautifully flexing and looks to be
Doing exactly what it is designed
For and it doesn't matter that the race

Is for show and that the mechanical
Rabbit is a contrivance to spur the
Hound to expend itself and it is not
Significant that there are other dogs

Competing alongside because I am
Watching this greyhound be a greyhound just
Like music is music and full of joy
And the race will be over soon enough

But it is only in the doing of
Life that things are properly realized.

The resting
afterwards is an
occasion for
reflection and
appreciation.

On a Sunday I was enjoying the
Southward view of the winding valley from
The elevated bluff of Pioneer
Park — I resolved to walk to the St. Croix

Crossing bridge far in the distance to the
South and I wanted to cross the span that
Was high above the river — to measure
The distance there and back with my feet — and

To see the river rippling below
The bridge — and I was curious about
The new walkway from Stillwater to the
Bridge — because there are many things I have

Never seen — and there were white butterflies
And I met a friend on a bicycle.

In about four
hours I returned to
the cherry tree in
Pioneer Park —
footsore.

The pulsation of waves coming in to
The shore as I was walking to the bridge
Was quicker than I supposed waves to be —
Then I remembered this is a river

And the waves were the result of a wake
From one of the boats on the river so
These were man-made emanations flowing
On the surface — and down the bank and through

The trees I could hear and glimpse the sight of
A jet skier bouncing on the water
And I imagined the freedom to leave
For anywhere on a whim and arrive

In a snap — but to me the jet skier
Was irritating like a mosquito.

The whine and the
impudence of the
coming and going
makes me a little
envious.

It was a little triumph to make it
To the bridge because it took more than an
Hour to arrive — but I considered
The walk a holiday because it was

Outside of my routine — and as I was
Ascending to a great height I saw the
Tallest cottonwoods by the shore below
Me — and the avenue of the bridge in

The sky seemed like a grand destination
With a walk-way for pedestrians and
With plaques at intervals explaining the
History of the frontier and of the

Watershed — of the nesting of eagles
And of the migration of tanagers.

I was rewarded
For years of
observation —
the new bridge
transformed the valley.

After resisting pressure to conform
To what everyone else is doing I
Joined Facebook — because I want to share my
Poems and sell books — and I entered the

Cyber world that is a carnival — with
Videos of performing animals
Photos of far away places and I
Reconnected with people I forgot

And I chatted with people in Bhutan
India and the Philippines and in
New Guinea — and I am barraged with friend
Requests from young women who are busting

Out of their clothes — who if they were here would
Probably not behave as they appear.

Out of touch
and far away —
what do these
women want?

I was driving and parked my car when my
Phone rang with an unusual jingle —
And I said hello and heard an Asian
Woman who I could not understand and

I heard a commotion that was hard to
Interpret but apparently there were
Two women conversing like birds and I
Think they are Chinese — they were giggling

And were waiting for a response from me
And I lowered the phone from my ear and
Saw two beautiful young women looking
At me because somehow they triggered the

Video capacity I never
Use — we blinked together and they vanished.

It was a summons
and a dismissal out of
the blue of Facebook
endlessly fascinating
and signifying nothing.

I have only been on Facebook for a
Few days and have no idea what the
Common experience is — my purpose
Is to promote books of poetry to

As large a potential readership as
Possible and I have found most of my
Friend requests come from adorable young
Women who are struggling to stay in

Their clothes — and I have more than five thousand
Such friends — but I don't if know the women
Are really women and if they really
Are beautiful or if they are sweaty

Guys in Pittsburg with schemes to extract as
As much money from me as possible.

I am a cyber
version of a Hollywood
celebrity with a
constant barrage of grasping
from people I don't know.

I imagine who I'm chatting with — and
There is only a photo to go
By — and it's not so easy — because my
Finger is blunt and it has to be placed

Exactly on the screen of my phone that
Doesn't leave room for error — but I am
Touching a person in cyber space with
Every tap of my finger and I will

Not tell a lie because one lie will have
To be followed by another and the
Terrible distortion of lying would
Effect my face to face behavior too

So I will pay attention to what moves
Me — and let my fingers play with the words.

Cyber space is a
window to the unbounded
imagination —
I have to be poised within
myself to be healthy.

There is sawdust covering the grass and
The hill — and there is a massive stump that
Is all that is left of the cottonwood —
And I won't see the craggy bark that was

The playground of squirrels — and there will be
No more sprays of seeds in the spring — and I
Won't be able to imagine that the
Turning leaves in a wind up and down the

Height of the tree are bells anymore — and
I will not measure the buoyancy of
The air by watching the floating of the
Cottonwood puffs in June either — but now

I will have to wear a wide brimmed hat at
My desk as a shield from the sunny glare.

I don't know why the
guy said they would grind
out the stump at no
additional cost —
they didn't grind it.

My thoughts and emotions resemble a
Magic fountain constantly arising
And on some days an event will turn the
Direction of my thinking — and sometimes

In idleness I do return to a
Habitual flow of thoughts that may be
Oppressive and punishing of myself —
And when I am sad it is helpful to

Be forgiving and gentle with myself
Because I cannot wrench myself into
A better way of thinking — but if there
Is the practice of kindness the fountain

Will again produce enthusiasm
As negativity does dissipate.

Enthusiasm is
natural — practice
letting negativity
dissipate with
kindness.

When I was taking the offerings from
The cat box out to the trash container
Kit escaped again — because I forgot
That he watches my every move — and in

The darkness about dawn I could barely
See him scampering with his tail in the
Air because Kit Cat is brown and blends with
Shadows — but I hurried and I suspect

He wants to be caught because he's afraid
Of the outdoors and he runs to make me
Chase and I always do catch him — which I
Couldn't do if he wanted his freedom —

When I march back home with him dangling
Limply in my hands he's not struggling.

The dark at that time
of my morning routine
impressed itself on
me — night is growing wings and
winter is coming again.

I had an important business meeting
And was nervous and in a hurry and
I got mail and left the post office and
To avoid a slowpoke in front of me

I looked in my rearview mirror and saw
Nothing so I turned the steering wheel right
And backed up and — smacked into a parked car —
I jumped out and there was damage on the

Driver's door and a big dent on my rear
Bumper — I didn't see anyone and
I could have left — my fourth accident in
Four years — oh my God — my insurance will

Triple quadruple — and I thought if I
Drove away now could I really escape?

I trudged next door
to the police station
to have a report made
and I met a beautiful
police woman.

Driving home last night with the windows of
The car open I heard the throbbing of
The crickets giving the air texture — this
Morning while I was meditating with

The windows open I noted that the
Darkness was creeping earlier into
The morning — and I heard a gentle rain
Hitting the roof and I noticed how the

Water sounds as it was running along
The gutters — there were little fears about
Attending to emails and changing the
Name and address on a checking account —

I lingered over a guy who is more than
An acquaintance and who is not a friend.

And then the impact
of the rain was fainter
and the light was
revealing the contents
of the room.

There is a little dot of green light that
Appears within the profile photo of
A person who uses the Messenger
App — and when the green dot is visible

The person is available to chat
At the moment — so if I want to talk
To Marilyn in the Philippines I
Type a message into a box on the

Screen and touch a pair of blue wings and my
Words are sent at the speed of light around
The Earth — Marilyn is having trouble
Falling asleep at night while the sun is

Rising here and something is bothering
Her but it's difficult to decipher.

There are glimmers
of personality
emotion and
an urge to control
in the use of words.

I was in the habit of coming to
My desk and window to watch the sunrise
And write poetry — but I joined Facebook
And accepted the friend requests of five

Thousand women with luscious photos — and
My phone buzzes with notifications
Of women from everywhere who want to
Chat with me from morning to night — and I

Juggle three conversations at once and
Fumble my typing and exchange photos
And chat face to face by video and
This new activity is distracting —

I am whirling in a cyber vortex
And am overlooking the sun and leaves.

I am a lonely
guy consuming
cotton candy
cyber
relationships.

I would love to go on vacation to
See the earth's highest tide at the Bay of
Fundy in Canada where the pull of
The moon on the ocean coming in and

Going out changes the depth of the sea
Over fifty feet — but I don't have the
Money or the time for a vacation —
So I will take the opportunity

In the spare moments of the day to look
For the little happenings about me
That I have never noticed before and
I will open my ears to the words of

My friends and savor the insights and the
Expressions coming with conversation.

I do not have to
go distances to
see the everyday
transformation of
this vivid moment.

A friend told me of an operation
Her mother is recovering from in
The hospital with the doctors and the
Nurses considering and balancing

The chemicals she needs — and the pace of
Her heart is monitored so that when she
Feels uncomfortable she can push a
Button and caretakers are alerted

At another location and they can
Adjust the flow of electrons needed
To stabilize the beating of her heart —
And her mother is disoriented

And wondering whether she has become
A machine dependant on technicians.

My friend said her
mother suffers because
her heart reflects the
burdens of people
in her life.

Facebook triggers my impulsivity
When I am driven to post my newest
Creation and don't want to take the time
To return to the poem in a few

Days to see whether I omitted words
Or could have made a more cogent point — and
After posting I become impatient
Returning to Facebook repeatedly

Throughout the day to see who has liked or
Commented on my poem as if I
Were seeking validation for myself —
And I am seeking for worthiness in

The ephemera of cyberspace — like
A teenager without experience.

Days or weeks later
someone I have never met
will comment on a
poem with unexpected
welcome reverberation.

There is rain without wind this morning and
The drumming of the rain through the windows
Punctuated my meditation and
The rain on the roof was tranquilizing

And now I am at my desk and looking
Out my window watching the rain descend
In a shower of tiny streaks that are
Only visible because of the green

Foliage of the trees — and I can see that
The gray sky the rain is falling from is
Glowing with a white light that reminds me
Even on a rainy day the sun is

Radiant — no matter what my troubles
Are simple observation is joyful.

The muggy heat of
last evening gave no hint
of the coolness and
the musical drops coming
and my bed sheets were sticky.

The I.R.S. became confused about
The name of my tax-exempt foundation
And the name of my magazine that is
Published by my tax-exempt foundation

Because my secretary used the wrong
Name on my paychecks — and my accountant
Sent a letter to the I.R.S. to
Alleviate the confusion and he

Said I had done nothing wrong and taxes
Were not owed — contrary to the claims of
Of the anonymous agents at the
I.R.S. — but I received a letter

Explaining that if I don't pay promptly
The agency will seize my property.

On this Labor Day
holiday weekend I am
thinking our letters
crossed in the mail and I am
determined not to worry.

The tallest waterfall on earth is called
The Angel Falls — it falls from a mountain range
In a South American jungle and
I will never see it except via

Video — but I can imagine the
River rushing between the rugged grey
Boulders and the water falling at the
Top into a quiet expanse of space

And I can see the dispersing droplets
Forming a mist subject to the wind and
I can appreciate the refraction
Of sunlight into a misty rainbow

And I can hear the impact of water
On water — a continuing marvel.

The falls were named after
Jimmy Angel whose puny
plane got stuck in the mud
on the mountain top — he
walked for eleven days
to find help.

I am lonely although usually
There is activity helping me to
Forget the fact of the loneliness — and
It is a thread of a woven garment

I am wearing in this lifetime — and while
There is much conversation and there are
Many companions to help me pass the
Time I am aware there is an absence

Where something needs to be — and I know how
To recognize the everyday trials and
Triumphs that are meaningful and I am
Able to generate the compassion

And the self-forgetting that could be love —
But something I don't know what is missing.

I am waiting
somehow to
articulate
and to absorb
intimacy.

He called this morning for the first time in
Over a year and we talked about the
Circles we go to that inspire our
Sobriety and enable us to

Turn around the negative attitudes
That can be dangerous — I spoke about
A similar gathering of people
Who address the afflictions of those who

Are related to alcoholics and
How it takes knowledgeable and focused
Effort to unlearn the coping skills of
Living with alcoholism as a

Child — and it is funny how a childhood
Interpretation does need correcting.

A child interprets
the craziness and neglect
of drunken parents
as justified punishment
for unlovable children.

I typed that she would be better off with
A younger guy nearby her — and I let
Go of her and went about my business —
But twenty minutes later my phone buzzed

And looking at my phone in my hand I
Saw her looking at me — and she is a
Beauty and knows that she is beautiful
And she is intelligent and crafty

With technology — her audacity
Was captivating and I was spellbound —
Many things are always happening at
The same time and there was an impact in

Our meeting face to face so suddenly —
Did I glimpse a vulnerability?

There can be such play
in the trading of words and
photos and video
and such anticipation —
what will I discover next?

The absence of the cottonwood outside
My window has continuing impact
As the cottonwood did so dominate
The view while I was putting my thoughts in

Order — and it was only on the odd
Day that the tree with craggy bark or the
Squirrels about the tree were the focus
Of my attention — but the tree was a

Fixture in the normalcy of life and
Now I am adjusting to the fact with
Fresh eyes — and a larger expanse of the
Sky is visible and the rising sun

Is more prominent and imposing and
Now the contrails of a jet are drifting.

The impact of
change is felt
suddenly and
gradually.

My friend who inherited a small farm
Told me of the differences from when
His father plowed with a team of horses —
The Department of Agriculture has

Mapped the taxability of every
Acre by using satellite data —
And the plowing and the harvesting are
Regulated by the government — and

Because corn is a world commodity
A farmer tending a small acreage
Is attentive to the tariffs between
America and China — and with the

Use of genetically modified
Crops lawsuits are disrupting the market.

Independence and
determination and brawn
aren't sufficient
anymore to operate
a cornfield in Iowa.

It takes a little exploration to
Realize most of the girls chatting on
Line over distances that make touching
Impossible are enticing men through

Words and photos and videos to give
Away their money — because so many
Are in the habit of chatting and are
So ingenious at attaching hooks

Into the psyche of men there must be
A mournful ocean of loneliness and
Addiction in cyberspace — though I know
How addiction deepens the loneliness

I did a little exploration but
I can't throw myself away so cheaply.

But Marilyn in
the Philippines
is genuinely
beautiful and
sweet.

From the view of Pioneer Park on a
Limestone bluff I could see the graceful lines
Of the St. Croix Crossing Bridge appearing
Tiny in the distance — and because it

Was a sunny Sunday and I was free
Of chores I decided to walk downtown
Stillwater and follow a walking path
By the river among the cottonwoods —

And on the way I took photos with my
Phone of the Lift Bridge in Stillwater with
The Crossing Bridge getting closer — and I
Sent the photos through the air to a girl

In Georgia and to another in the
Philippines to share in my adventure.

I ascended from
the riverbank and walked in
the sunlight towards the
gargantuan Crossing Bridge
anticipating marvels.

Starting out on the walking way over
The bridge the tallest cottonwoods on the
River bank were below me — and a mile
Ahead of me on the other side of

The bridge the people walking looked tiny
And as I was walking over the span
That crosses the valley and river at
A great height I listened to the cars and

Trucks and motorcycles passing in both
Directions and I noticed the waves of
Sound rose to a crescendo coming to
Me and diminished going away — and

The sound of traffic nearby or in the
Distance makes me feel a little lonely.

People move
together separately
continuously
transporting
solitary lives.

The sights and sounds on a day of walking
Are part of the event — and there is the
Exploration of hopes and desires
Or the reckless exercise of complaints

But the pleasure of walking for me is
The liberation of consciousness and
The discovery of meaning — and the
Words of Cid Corman returned to me from

Thirty years ago — and he said I should
Live my poetry — and maybe he meant
I should be sincere and generous and
That my words would be a reflection of

My spirit or perhaps he meant something
Else — but I do aim for sincerity.

Returning from the
Crossing Bridge striding the last
slope with aching feet
I felt the mild declining
sun with satisfaction.

The light on the leaves in the morning is
Golden in September and the air is
Crisp and if there were a time within the
Seasons that I would like to extend it

Would be September because the sun is
Not glaring and the afternoon heat is
Gentle — there are a few trees in town that
Are turning yellow and red but green is

Predominate and throughout the day when
A breeze is in the trees the light on the
Turning leaves is golden — that serves as a
Signal that now is the culmination

Of growth and a harvest is approaching
And then the days will become desolate.

I remember how
wind tosses leaves
in spring — there is a
boisterous joy.

The season for roses has passed this year
But when thinking about you roses come
To mind — because you are blooming in the
Sunny springtime of your life and you do

Approximate the velvet folds within
Folds that constitute a rose — and the moon
Has a mysterious allure because
Of its various shapes and colors and

Its movements — and the sun is marvelous
Because it is the resplendent source of
Breath and life — but you as you are now are
The epitome of beauty and love

Forcefully drawing me to you as if
I were under a spell and mesmerized.

Passion for
possession
is consuming
and thorns are
a warning.

The cherry in September is just such
A humble little tree surrounded by
The taller and broader trees reaching up
And out spreading their leaves — taking so much

More sunlight — and here is the maple in
Pioneer Park beginning to show the
Touches of orange that will become so
Brilliant in October — and Pioneer

Park is just a tiny area of
Stillwater on a bluff overlooking
The valley with a southward view of the
Turning river with the Crossing Bridge in

The distance — and Stillwater is just a
Modest town in a boisterous nation.

But when the cherry
is blooming in spring
its beauty is just
unsurpassable.

Of the unnumbered things I could have seen
On my walk from home over the Crossing
Bridge and back again I saw a yellow
Bird hopping among branches — and by the

River the wind was visible when a
Hawk was gliding and circling — and the
Broad surface of the water between the
Banks was undulating separately

From the current and bobbing a tied barge —
And from the view at the height of the bridge
Shadows of clouds were moving on the trees
On both sides of the river — and on the

Way back under the cottonwoods I heard
A cricket punctuate the afternoon.

The Crossing Bridge from
Pioneer Park looks tiny —
I have measured the
distance with my feet there and
back — three and a half hours.

Taking account of what an addict does
Watching the behavior and trying to
Understand why the addict doesn't have
A common sense of self-respect that

Should prevent the stupid indulgence of
Temporary pleasure — when the certain
Consequences are terrible and
It's easy to see the bitterness and

Remorse afterwards — it is confounding
To witness the continuation of
Addiction — as addiction inspires
The disgust and repulsion of people

Who used to be friends — and the family
Is exhausted with useless excuses.

Only another
addict who has
sobriety can put
the puzzle pieces
together.

The momentum of the downward spiral
Was baffling as the people who cared
Lacked the power to influence addiction
And I really had no explanation

Because the ecstasy of the drug had
Vanished and there was no longer any
Pleasure or escape in the addiction —
But I was willing to do anything

To turn my life around — and I did by
By listening to addicts who thought and
Felt and behaved like me — and I might not
Have done it if the situation had

Not arrived when the effective words were
Said with kindness to pierce my denial.

I did not know that
I was dying until
the desperation
was revealed to me
by other addicts.

Sadly Kit Cat is too clever for his
Own good and he is expert at waiting
For the few seconds when the door opens —
And when it was time to feed the cats at

Noon yesterday Johnnie and Henry were
Present but Kit was nowhere in the house
And I could only surmise that he went
Out when I did without me noticing

Because that's the only explanation —
And a downpour began in the morning
And a heavy rain continued during
The day and Kit Cat was nowhere to be

Found — so as clever as he is he chose
The absolutely worst day to escape.

I laid awake in bed
with memories of Kit Cat's
absurdities and
antics hoping he has the
common sense to return home.

It is unnatural to keep a cat
Within a house for a lifetime when a
Cat is intended to use the stalking
Waiting and pouncing skills it was born with

And Kit Cat is much like a miniature
Mountain lion who I would notice at the
Window everyday alertly watching
And listening outdoors — and so his urge

To escape is irrepressible and
Honorable and perhaps I'm being
Too possessive in my concern but I
Am worrying about where he is in

The rain whether he can elude the dogs
And will he be able to return home?

About 4 a.m.
a familiar utterance
came through the window —
I went out to meet Kit Cat
and he was completely dry.

Every Saturday throughout the year we
Gather for morning meditation — and
In between our sitting meditation
We stand up and leave the cozy chapel

Within the church and enter the roomy
Sanctuary where the stained glass windows
Filter the sunlight of the season — and
With a clear bell we begin walking in

A meditative fashion stepping and
Carefully attending to the rising
And placing of our feet and breathing in
With the rising and breathing out with the

Falling of every step harmonizing
Motion and letting our mind waves ripple.

There is a balance
of motion and thought —
attending to what
we do everyday
with a bit more care.

I am what I give my attention to
This morning and I am dwelling on a
Person who is not quite a friend and am
Considering the friction between us

That I believe is based on differing
Opinions and on a rivalry for
Dominance within a circle of friends —
And I hold my thoughts gently within the

Oval my hands are making as my hands
Are resting motionless on my lap as
I am meditating with my legs crossed
With my back straight — and I am giving my

Mind the freedom to show me the burdens
It has so I can let them dissipate.

I accept my
perceptions may be
an imagined
contrivance so
I hold them gently.

When holding my thoughts within the oval
I am making with my hands as I am
Meditating in the morning I am
Gentle with myself — and when money and

Bills come to mind I recognize fear and
Let it go — and when criticism of
People arises there is the urge to
Control that in time dissipates — and my

Hands do not become fists — and I do not
Grasp and fling my disturbance away — but
I am determinedly patient and hold
My thoughts gently letting my thoughts arise

And disappear because my thoughts are like
Smoke vanishing into a vast sky.

The crossing of my
legs and the discipline of
keeping my back straight
serve to position my mind
to reveal life's combustion.

When I am quiet and determined to
Sit for a length of time without moving
I am willing to let my thoughts arise
Without interference — and I may be

Angry with someone — or I may be so
Nervous about a situation which
I can't control — and it is really hard
To sit quietly and discover the

Depth of my emotion — but I resolved
To sit quietly for a length of time
And it is a worthy practice to let
The power of my emotions arise

So that I engage with the magnitude
And grow some moxie by facing the truth.

Energy builds
energy transforms
and alters
perceptions.

There is a quiet joy in learning how
To harmonize my energy — so that
I can encourage the activity
I love when I have the clarity of

Mind to do it — going to sleep early
Enough to wake early enough when
The neighborhood is quiet enough so
That I can enjoy the playing with thoughts

That my mind does enthusiastically
Is a method of starting the day that
Took almost sixty years to discover —
Without haste and distraction I wake up

And assume a meditative posture
And my thoughts will bloom into gentle hands.

When distraction and
haste overcomes me
occasionally
an underlying
quiet is present.

I know it is time to trim my nails when
One of them cracks and causes discomfort
When I am putting in or taking out
Something from my pocket — and because I

Am left handed I do a better job
Clipping the nails of my right hand and I
Can generate tremendous and skillful
Leverage filing down the sharp edges to

A pleasing smoothness — but when I apply
The clipper to my left fingers with my
Right hand it is a tricky endeavor
And I am never a slap dash person

But for my left hand I will make due with
A little less propitious result.

The little toe on
my left foot is
hard — I twist it
with my right hand — aim —
and clip.

My eyes are

insightful

my arms are

handy and

my legs are

footy.

Vietnam

The French occupied Indochina
A century before the Second World
War and during the war the Japanese
Invaded and the Vietnamese starved —

And the Viet Minh arose to expel
The invaders with guerrilla warfare —
And American agents provided
Arms and training and the Americans

Admired Vietnamese patriots
Because the Americans remembered
Their colonial history — after the
War the French returned to repossess their

Colony and the French leader De Gaulle
Demanded American compliance.

The French would help
America fight Communists
in Europe — if
America were neutral
in French Indochina.

Marxism offers equality and
Economic freedom as long as the
Individual surrenders private
Property and accepts the leadership

Of the Vanguard — and in the twentieth
Century the Communists had their chance
In the revolutions they began to
Impose their system — and in the twenty-

First century it is apparent there
Never was a more idealistic
Form of government that created as
Many corpses as the Communists did —

In the Black Book of Communism the
Low estimate is one hundred million.

Half the world was
frightened to death of
the Communist
revolutionaries who
were transforming nations.

An individual can embody
The contradictions the sympathies and
The inspiration of many people
And so when trying to understand the

Heroic essence of Ho Chi Minh who
Led the Vietnamese to expel the
French from Vietnam it is important
To take account of the motivation

He instilled in his people — was it his
Marxist ideology imported
From foreigners or a Vietnamese
Yearning to rid the country of foreign

Occupation that fired the hearts of
His people and compelled self-sacrifice?

The American
presidents and generals
said America
was saving Vietnam from
Communist domination.

Divine omniscience takes account of
History and culture and spirit but
Americans were scared of atom bombs
And Communist expansion throughout the

Earth and with the passage of time it is
Easy to see that the Vietnamese
Communists were never a threat to the
American homeland but presidents

Were compelled to oppose Marxism in
Proxy nations with limited warfare
Involving ambush and sabotage and
Calculated escalation always

With the prevention of atomic war
In mind with the Russians and the Chinese.

The presidents
Kennedy Johnson Nixon
were probably right —
reelection depended
on fighting Communism.

The American military aimed
To win the hearts and minds of the people
Of South Vietnam by supporting a
Series of corrupt and unpopular

Vietnamese leaders in Saigon — and
American soldiers conducted search
And destroy missions in South Vietnam
Confronting the Viet Cong and the North

Vietnamese Army — and marauding
Americans uprooted people and
Burned hamlets and rice — and Americans
Blundered into ambushes and booby

Traps in rice paddies and elephant grass
And in the sweltering hilly jungle.

Americans
encountered
passivity
during the day and
enemies at night.

The war in Vietnam coincided
With the evolution of civil rights
In America when Americans
Were struggling with the inequities

Between the blacks and people of lighter
Color and it became more apparent
As the war progressed that the blacks and the
Poor — the people who prospered the least — were

More likely to be drafted and wounded
And killed because they lacked the privileges
Of the wealthy — and it was obvious
That the South Vietnamese as the war

Dragged didn't like being uprooted and
Resented American foreigners.

The Vietnamese
were forced from the countryside
into city slums —
they saw the corruption of
profiteering generals.

Only after the passage of decades
When the people who made the decisions
Were safely dead were the memoranda
Of the presidents revealed in a

Documentary that demonstrates that
Kennedy and Johnson and Nixon and
The top advisors McNamara and
Kissinger from the beginning were

Aware that victory was doubtful but
They kept sending Americans soldiers
To assault another meaningless hill in
The jungle and when the hill was taken

The soldiers left it behind and they took
The bodies of their dead — in most cases.

The enemy died
at a rate of ten to one
American death
so victory was assured
General Westmoreland said.

The America people did not want
To believe that President Johnson and
General Westmoreland would ever be
Dishonest about the war but when the

Enemy suddenly assaulted so
Much South Vietnamese territory
On the morning of the Tet Offensive
It was revealed that the American

Strategy was not effective and that
The enemy was quite ferociously
Determined — and then the American
Public began to realize there was

A difference between what they were told
And what was happening in Vietnam.

Limited war in
Vietnam was becoming
ugly and senseless
and Americans perceived
their leaders were lying.

The war in Vietnam impacted on
American society like a
Hammer shattering a framed mirror — and
The frame keeps the shards from falling out — but

Ever since the war we see ourselves as
Divided factions quite suspicious of
Each other — when we separate into
Racial and ethnic and class rivalries —

And when we are confronted by hostile
Forces beyond our borders we argue
Whether we are the cause of the conflict
Whether we have a right to self-defense

Or whether on balance we are a good
Nation seeking for a proper response.

The Vietnam War
reminds Americans
sometimes politicians
are less than truthful and
vigilance is important.

It is fitting that the Vietnam War
Memorial is near America's
Capitol building and the White House and
Arlington Cemetery and it is

Very peaceful with shady trees and a
Gently sloping lawn — the memorial
Dispenses with the airs of triumph that
Often typify a nation's symbols —

It is a wall of black granite with the
Names of soldiers who died sacrificing
Themselves for the good of America
Inscribed in stone so that loved ones can reach

Out and touch the names of those they lost — and
Hopefully we will grow humility.

If war memorials
were required to inscribe
all the names of those
who die would we
have fewer wars?

Vietnam hints
perhaps we may not
comprehend everything
we think we know.

— *Tekkan*

Everyday Mind IX

The harvest moon
was large and orange
on the horizon —
it is small and silver
this morning.

I knew that people needed bifocals
When they get older but I believed that
My eyes wouldn't be effected — but then
I became irritated with the small

Printing of the books I was reading and
My eyes began to hurt from looking at
A computer screen at work — and now I
Occasionally close my eyes and rest while

Listening to my surroundings knowing
What aging feels like and accepting that
Sometimes the world will appear blurred and
Watery to me until my eyesight

Sharpens again as I am learning how
To pace the use of my abilities.

Birds clouds
autumn leaves
the warm expressions
of my friends are
more precious.

I've gotten used to being present and
Listening while a group is having a
Lively conversation because it does
Happen that they have more in common with

Each other then I do with them — and I've
Put up with the discomfort that comes with
Feeling separate from people — but I
Am refining my morning clarity

When I settle with my desk and keyboard
Along with my containers of coffee
And I play with perceptions by finding
The words that fit well together and in

The play there is a hunt for worthiness —
There is something worth articulating.

Within the
ordinary
there is the
extraordinary.

I knew it was the last time that I would
Meet with Zen Master Harada at a
Temple in the town of Obama on
A bay by the Sea of Japan because

I was returning to America —
And we were sitting on the tatami
Together in the Japanese style for
Our last words — and my abdomen filled with

A sudden warmth as we faced each other
And the warmth originated from the
Zen Master as he demonstrated the
Love and power of the emptiness from

Which everything arises — and thirty
Years later the warmth resides within me.

There are times when I
forget the inspiration
of that moment but
there is a connection now
that can never be broken.

I was surprised this morning by the frost
That needed to be scraped from my windshield
Because I was in a hurry and was
Not prepared to have the time taken from

Me — and on my way around town I see
The party colors of the autumn leaves
Emerging and already the season
Is cooler while spring seemed to have arrived

Yesterday — and at home I will raise the
Screen windows and lower the outward glass
So that the double panes of glass of each
Window are in place for the winter cold —

I won't need the dehumidifier
But will have to rely on the furnace.

An air of
seriousness
and severity
is settling
over Stillwater.

There is always a horizon in the
Distance and the permutations of the
Sky are continuous — and I am not
Separate from this overcast morning

But the gloom is counterbalanced with the
Yellow and orange and scarlet leaves — and
I remember tulips by the garage
The apple blossoms by the driveway and

The lilacs on the corner and it seems
Like yesterday I was measuring the
Amount of shoveling necessary with
My first step out of the door and into

The snow and the snow was heavy and deep
And I knew that I would be struggling.

The break from the rain
the dampness in the air and
the gray of the sky
from which the water will drop
are a weight upon my mind.

It is ironic that in English the
Word "hole" beginning with the letter
"H" represents a nothingness and yet
The word "Whole" beginning with the letter

"W" — a doubling of a "u" —
Indicates something that is complete and
Harmonious within itself — so that
The same sound spelled differently indicates

Both absence and an inclusive presence —
And it is evocative that in the
Middle of the Milky Way there is a
Black hole with enough gravity to spin

A hundred billion stars about itself
At one point three million miles per hour.

The Buddhists say
in emptiness there is form
and in form there is
emptiness.

The grass is soaked with overnight rain and
The sky has been overcast this morning
But the clouds are separating and the
Sun is appearing and disappearing

As we are in the twilight time of the
Seasons again on the verge of longer
Nights and for me the quality of light
Becomes precious — as just for a moment

I saw the edges of a bank of clouds
Lit by the sun before a mass of gray
Obscured my view — and it is true even
In winter I cannot look directly

At the sun without damaging my eyes
But I will enjoy the reflected sun.

The leaves are in
autumn colors
and aren't falling
yet but it is
inevitable.

I am doing what is possible to
Expand my circle of acquaintance and
Now that I've composed several books and want
To market them I am meeting poets

At poetry readings where we share each
Others' vision and enthusiasm —
And this group meets once a month and perhaps
I'm off balance and assuming too much

But I sense guardedness amongst us as
If we were competing for attention
And status of ability were up
For grabs — and I want admiration —

But I'm also lonely and looking for
Companions and lively exploration.

Every single day
there is something worth
remembering and
communication
aids intuition.

Today I am enjoying my little
Bubble of consciousness on a rainy
Day in October by imagining
Piles of snow along the streets as I am

Driving to meet my circle of sober
Alcoholics — because I know there will
Be an hour of honest and healthy
Discussion — and no matter what gloomy

Encumbrance I arrive with I know
From experience my troubles will melt
Away once I sit among companions
And practice listening and when it is

My turn to speak with the intention of
Being positive I am positive.

Enthusiasm
is easier with
companions and
with ears.

The key to my Japanese car does have
A blade that would fit in the keyway of
The door but I have never used my key
That way — instead I push a button and

Waves emanate from the key and unlock
The door automatically — and in the
Morning and evening I am sending
Text messages and photos to a friend in

Sri Lanka by touching the screen of my
Phone with my fingers and through the air my
Thoughts and emotions and the images
I like arrive instantaneously

Around the earth — and I am waking up
In bed and she is in the evening.

Emotions are
sticky and
digestion and
comprehension
are tricky.

It is already cold enough to chill
In the early days of October and
The wind has a biting edge and the swift
Gray clouds are coalescing into an

Overcast sky of impending storm but
Most of the leaves haven't fallen and I
Haven't cut and bagged the daylilies and
Hostas and haven't mowed the grass for a

Final time — I am accustomed to the
Timely passage of leaves and I enjoy
The regularity of my outside
Chores as if by emptying gas from the

Lawn mower and by changing the oil in
The snow blower I am really ready.

The leaves are
brilliantly colored —
and soon the wind
will be howling through
the bare branches.

My mind is a bowl I am holding in
My hands attending to the arising
Of my thinking — and the politics of
Today is poisonous with villains and

Saviors and battles without end — and I
Am digesting detailed controversy
Desiring the triumph of goodness
Witnessing emotional distortions

And flammable opinions without the
Possibility of moderation —
And I am organizing my point of
View and marshalling an array of facts

To satisfy an urge for clarity
But I am also wanting a release.

While cutting and bagging
daylilies and hostas
in preparation for
winter I will gently
dissipate bitterness.

I will pluck all of the apples from the
Tree that I can reach and let the others
Fall to feed the squirrels — and I will seize
The Hostas and daylilies and cut and

Bag them — my legs will give me leverage
My back and arms will be pulling — my right
Hand will grasp — and my left will slice with
A bright steel blade — and tomorrow my legs

And back will punish me and I will have
Difficulty moving for several
Days — and after the exuberance of
Activity has worn off my fingers

Will ache and the swollen areas will
Inform me where splitters are embedded.

When I am cutting
and bagging I will seize this
sunny afternoon
to indulge vibrant and
exhilarated thinking.

The African elephants have floppy
Ears while Asian elephants have tiny
Ears but both the African and Asian
Elephants can detect the lumbering

Presence of far away elephants by
"Listening" to the plodding of thudding
Elephant feet emanating in the
Waves from every elephant foot that stomps

On the earth — but the elephant doesn't
Hear elephants thumping with its ears but
It measures the distance of its plopping
Cousins through the bottom of its feet as

It stands in place tickled by vibrations
Stimulating its marvelous flatness.

The wrinkles around
an elephant's eyes suggest
wisdom but with its
wrapping and grasping trunk it
behaves mischievously.

The destroying edge of the eye wall of
A hurricane wrenches a broad swath of
Habitation — but the narrow focus
Of a tornado is personal when

A family's home is ripped apart but a
Neighbor's is not — and the downpour of a
Hurricane saturates the valleys and
Floods the streets and homes with enveloping

Devastation — bringing sudden change — but
Such lightning fractures are not the subjects
Of my poetry because they haven't
Happened to me and so how could I be

Authentic in description — so I will
Write about the cumulative changes.

There is an
accumulation of
snow this morning
with the leaves resolutely
clinging to the trees.

Because the cats are so insistent I
Feed them right after waking up in the
Morning but today I changed the routine
And brushed them beforehand and they made the

Same noise as always — and I am used to
Doing my chores in regular order —
But I am discovering the order
Is arbitrary and I am doing

What I want in another sequence in
The same amount time — if I shave and
Shower before breakfast I won't be late —
And once I am soaping under a stream

Of clarifying water my thinking
Will reveal what is important today.

Often I am
exuberant but
sometimes there is
an urgency
to succeed.

I've been trying to explain with thousands
Of words the experience of seeking
For inspiration in ordinary
Events so very easy to discount

And I believe it was necessary
For me to cross a threshold of pain and
Dissatisfaction — and I was lucky
To realize my spirit was growing

Under the pressure of adversity —
And I was surprised that my bitterness
Was dissolving when I joined a circle
Of friends and I began listening to

How they turned their difficulties over
To wisdom surpassing comprehension.

So much trouble
comes from wanting
what I really
don't need.

With the passage of the several months
Since the removal of the cottonwood
Outside the window where I assemble
My thoughts into words on paper I can

See so much more sunrise pouring over
The neighboring trees — the light is slanting
Across my view and lighting the leaves from
An angle and leaving most of the trees

In shadow — the light is mixing with the
Autumn colors and where it is touching
The leaves passing through a blue sky there is
Joyous brilliance that lightens my heart and

Miles away I can enjoy the tiny
White contrails of a jetliner drifting.

Within two weeks the
leaves will be down and through
bare branches the far
edge of the river valley
will become visible.

This room where I work is disorganized
With things that are no longer useful to
The operation of the business like
The envelope collating machine and

The light table for laying out copy
To be printed — and there are cobwebs in
The corners of the windows and dust is
Collecting on the books in the shelves — but

The light coming into the windows and
Illuminating the hundreds of things
And the light revealing the ten thousand
Things within sight outside of the windows

Every day is the light enlivening
Everything that ever lived on the earth.

In daylight there is
an overlay of
stimulation and
vibrancy easy
to overlook.

Today we are experiencing the
Twilight season of the year preparing
For the months when the wind is howling in
The bare branches and snow has overcome

The ground but that is not what's happening
Now as I am walking by the river
Over the Crossing Bridge and back to my
Home in Stillwater — I am watching the

Afternoon sun sparkle among the red
And yellow and orange leaves in a breeze
And the leaves are falling in the breeze and
This will be my last long walk when it is

Possible this year to see a golden
Burst of the sun flicker among the leaves.

Everyday
more light and
vitality
is draining
from daylight.

I was watching a video on my
Phone of a juvenile elephant in
A creek with muddy and slippery banks —
The youngster wanted out and came to a

Sloping spot and not too steep — and thrusting
Upwards and flopping sideways onto the
Bank the elephant reached a tipping point
Several times but just couldn't get over —

Looking like a chubby kid struggling
Up the wall on an obstacle course and
Failing — in befuddlement and distress
The adolescent wavered in the creek

Until an adult ambling over
And stepping into the creek helped him out.

The elephant
used his massive
head to push
from behind and
they escaped.

The branches are brown under a gray sky
And drops of rain are falling here and there
Into the grass that is sodden and green —
And red and yellow leaves are on the street

And I am seeing the birds frolicking
In the air as a group turning in an
Instant and stopping in a bare tree — and
Then they fly again turning together

As if they were of one mind and then they
Vanish — and the last leaves are descending
Singly and severally in the wind
And I can see a rainy haze on the

Horizon across the river valley —
And it is not cold enough to snow yet.

The birds frolic
as if the gray sky
were not concerning
and air and branches
were eternal.

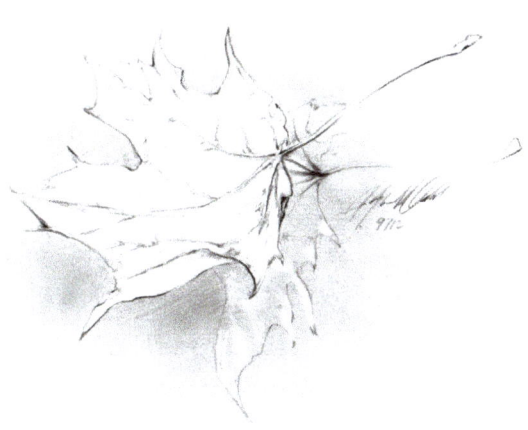

It's perplexing that in the transition
Into winter there is a blooming of
Vibrancy when the white and grey of a
Cloud rapidly blowing in the blue of

The sky makes a stunning contrast — when just
Moments ago the finest flakes of snow
Were descending — and I question why when
The leaves of each tree are revealing the

Most brilliant yellows oranges and reds
Something irrepressible inside me
Awakens with joyful celebration
As if today were a festival of

Natural beauty — while my bare hands are
Chilled to the bone by a persisting wind.

It happens that the
severity of winter
is proceeded by
a reverberation of
exuberant piquancy.

When a problem without an emerging
Solution is in my way I don't have
To worry because soon I will cross my
Legs and meditate — and I don't sit with

The intention of solving my problems
And there is the freedom to think about
Whatever I want — but I have come to
Enjoy watching my thoughts in transition

And energy envelopes my thinking
And transforms my inclinations over
Time so when a persisting conundrum
Or an emotional snare arises

I am good at regaining my balance
Because I have dissolving energy.

Releasing
energy
underlies
experience
transforming
experience.

There is a cottonwood on the corner
Of my yard that drops its leaves later than
The other surrounding trees on the cusp
Of November — and a quarter of the

Leaves have fallen but it will take a week
For all of them to go — and this morning
The slanting light caught the yellow leaves and
Produced a glowing orange and there was

Not any wind — I was leaving home on
The way to work thinking about how to
Apportion the chores that need doing with
My limited time including raking

The cottonwood leaves and bagging leaves for
The waste disposal pickup on Thursday.

The yellowest leaves
on a frosty morning were
suffused in slanting
transitory sunlight but
now the sight is vanishing.

Apart from the persona I assume
When composing my poems I do have
A nervous disposition as I rush
From one chore to another — and there are

Emails to read and write and essays to
Consider once I'm done with laundry
And cooking eating and washing dishes —
And the once in a while intrusions — like

Calling the accountant and maintaining
The car and raking leaves — are as constant
As clouds drifting along in the sky — but
When I'm attending to the clouds I am

Serene though when doing chores I can be
Resentfully harassed and distracted.

I can also be
the juggler with
busy hands tossing
my chores
happily.

Yesterday I communicated with
You about being just too jittery and
Distracted and I could not have written
Otherwise because I was in the midst

Of unavoidable bustle with not
Enough time in the day — and the haste of
The moment had to be balanced by the
Need to choose my words carefully — and the

Words came with difficulty but they fell
Into place eventually so that
Even though I hurried through the rest of
The day I could cherish a smidgen of

Satisfaction because in difficult
Circumstances I did find expression.

I can't wrench
myself into peaceful
thinking — but I
can learn to surf
turbulent emotions.

It wouldn't be correct to believe that
I am a master of myself because
That would suggest that serenity comes
Easily to me — but at least when I

Am nervous I recognize nervousness —
When conflicted with many thoughts going
In too many directions I do know
At the moment it would be better if

I could slow down a little — and I am
Surprised by the strength of my emotions
But I don't try to ignore or suppress
Them anymore and if I am careful

Even in the midst of activity
I can resonate with satisfaction.

I respond to
circumstances
and am better
at regaining
composure.

There was rain and wind in the night and in
The morning most of the leaves were on the
Ground and seeing the newly bare branches
Again is a stark indication of

The bleak season before us but I will
Use several afternoons to rake and bag
The leaves as active meditation to
Reflect during the exercise of my

Body on what I am doing now that
Increases my dissatisfaction — I
Usually know if I am honest
With myself when I am doing something

That can only lead to unhappiness
And what would be a better direction.

Pulling the rake
clearing the ground
collecting the leaves
bending and bagging
gathering willingness.

When the bare branches are revealed in
In the pale blue sky of a cold morning
And the light is brilliant in the leaves of
A few trees that are holding on for the

Last hour I savor a melancholy
Pleasure in the draining away of the
Vibrancy of summer — and the birds that
Were singing with the rising sun are gone —

And the grass isn't growing — and the leaves
That were yellow a few days ago on
My cottonwood were brown on the ground — and
Now they are in bags along the street to

Be disposed of — today I have only
One blister on my hand from raking leaves.

But a blue sky is
always full of light
and even on a
cold overcast day
I generate warmth.

I know the sun is ninety-three million
Miles away and gravity is crushing
Inward on the core and resulting in
Nuclear fusion and combustion and

A photon of light and energy is
Colliding with other photons for ten
Million years before it emerges from
The core to the surface of the sun — and

It only takes eight minutes to reach the
Earth — and I know every living being
On the earth lives by the grace of the sun
And the sun has always been a giver

Of warmth and life and consciousness even
On a cloudy day in early winter.

It is the same
radiance on my
cottonwood that
moved people to build
Stonehenge.

The crows are always in the trees or on
The ground in threes or fours by the carcass
Of a rabbit in the grass or stabbing
A dead squirrel on the road — and they will

Fly away as I drive by — and I do
Hear their harsh voices coming in the open
Windows in the summer and imagine
The imposition of dominance in

Crow language — but when the leaves are down and
The branches are starkly bare again their
Black presence in the trees or on the ground
Reveals the return of the barren days

When the sunlight is less prominent and
And an icy wind is in the branches.

There is
austere beauty
in the rising sun
in the bare branches.

Chickadees are messy eaters he said
And he has two tubular feeders in
His yard and the chickadees empty one
A week — and he will be working in the

Yard and they will be flitting back and forth
But when he looks at them they will stop and
Scatter — he lives in a wooded hollow
And in the winter he sees chickadees

Nut hatches yellow-bellied sapsuckers
Sparrows pileated woodpeckers and
Cardinals — and he is ambling through
His days and aware of how lucky he

Is because where I go there are only
The crows stabbing carcasses on the street.

Before the sunrise
a pink light is along the
horizon beyond the
river valley visible
because the leaves have fallen.

It happens at the gym with people I
See now and then after saying hello
To each other for months finally we
Introduce ourselves and I walk away

Grateful to have made another friend and
Then the days or weeks go by without our
Meeting — but then I see him again and
Realize I can't remember his name

So I scurry out of sight before he
Sees me — and I don't want him to suppose
His name is not worthy enough of
My remembering it — and I am so

Ashamed of myself for my forgetting
But there is no getting around the fact.

And it happens at
the gym that sometimes I can
remember someone's
name and they are forgetting
mine — and I am quite relieved.

Eventually my forgetting of
A name needs to be remedied because
I am on friendly terms with everyone
So I make an admission and I hear

The name repeated and I resort to
Tricks — sometimes I may connect a person
With the name of a famous person or
With a friend who has the very same name —

And sometimes I may identify a
Prominent feature such as with Nosey
Nolan or Boisterous Bob — but then it's
Imperative that I remember though

Perhaps my earnest effort doesn't help
And makes remembering more difficult.

I also try to
suppress thoughts
inadvertently
producing
obsession.

There is a bush warbler in Japan I
Heard while walking along a mountain path
In spring — and I never saw the bird but
Its sound was a liquid loveliness that

Was otherworldly — and the Japanese
Call it the *uguisu* and the name
Is an attempt to recreate its song
But that is impossible to do with

Syllables because the warbler doesn't
Repeat a pattern and people aren't birds
And every instance the *uguisu*
Sings the sound is a once-in-a-lifetime

Penetration of the day and thirty
Years later I remember its effect.

I recall the
vaguest memory of
fascination.

The *uguisu* was hidden in my
Memory until I read a volume
Of poetry by Ryokan who was
A Japanese Zen monk who lived in a

Hermitage in the mountains and who wrote
That his poems were not poems — and when
He described sitting by a banana
Tree that seemed to be sweeping clouds away

And cooling his hut with shade he conveyed
The moment with an uncluttered heart and
He wasn't thinking about practicing
Zen but he was immersed in reading the

Wordless verses of nature absorbing
Drifting illusion and enlightenment.

The sound of the
uguisu happens
as everything
is arising
at once.

The aftermath of an election is
A revelation every time when the
Winning coalitions and strategies
Are determined and the operatives

Can never be secure by deploying
Superior knowledge or gamesmanship
Because the voting public is fickle
And emotion and loyalty can shift

And once a person assumes a point of
View in every national election
Virtuous candidates lose and scoundrels
Prevail in some locations — and it is

Necessary that the voters bear the
Consequences and hopefully they learn.

Snow is covering
the bare branches this morning
so I put on a
wool hat and boots and mittens
and a warm winter jacket.

It would be easy in November to
Let the imposition of a gray sky
Overwhelm my outlook without even
Being consciously aware of the shift

In my attitude — going about my
Business I settle into the drab browns
Of the trees without their leaves with the thin
Layer of the first snow on the ground and

With the sudden arrival of the cold
That clings to every movement I make when
Without noticing much I calculate
Whether gloves are necessary while I'm

Handling thermoses of coffee and
Aiming the key to turn and lock my door.

The experience
of a gray November sky
settling upon
my mind imposing the cold
again is worth noticing.

From one day to the next things may appear
Differently and this morning the branches
Have a coating of snow and the sky is
White with just a tinge of gray — and behind

My home there is a birch that throughout the
Summer I seldom notice because its
White bark is overwhelmed by the sun and
The grass and leaves and the blue of the sky

And there is always a dog barking and
The birds are about — but in the stillness
Of morning the white paper birch blends in
With its brown branches and twigs and with the

Snow on the ground it epitomizes
The beauty of a quiet winter day.

Tromping along
after the first snowfall
and making my first
boot prints in the snow I am
pioneering the landscape.

A friend sent a book of Buddhist wisdom
From Sri Lanka and last evening I read
Much familiar *dharma* — and I liked the
Perspective that science may dissect the

Material world but has no leverage
Over the dynamics of the mind and
Consciousness — and I was reminded of
The necessity of understanding the

Law of karma that I must live with the
Consequences of my predilections
But when I woke this morning I recalled
Her point — we can't purify the world we

Can only purify ourselves — and the
Urge to dominate causes suffering.

For twenty-five years
I've been editing a
political journal
chastising peoples'
mischievous behavior.

The gift of inspiration is the best
That we may give each other and I am
Capable of giving after having
My measure of suffering and after

Having some insight into the cause of
The suffering — and I am grateful to
Have my circle of friends and the room where
We meet — and I am lucky we practice

Our listening without interruption
And it does take practice to understand
The turning points that warped the lens I use
For seeing and if I do carefully

Listen then I may recognize enough
Similarity and be insightful.

Honesty without
the imposition of
advice is sufficient
for receiving clarity
and creating gratitude.

There is a book about recovery
From addiction and alcoholism
With many fine expressions and words well
Worth the reading about what it means to

Have a spirit capable of growing
Beyond the grasping and frightened ego
But for me the best thing about the book
Is the photo on the cover of an

Asphalt road turning within a forest
With the sunlight bursting in the trees and
Symbolizing the glowing fact of life
That I may choose to pursue a path that

Is founded on the assumption of a
Goodness that I may grow my roots into.

The choice is mine
whether to allow
parasitic thoughts and
lethargy to consume me
or to follow the way.

There is a trick that goes on in the
Political world that's great for gaining
Leverage and momentum and that is
To assume self-righteousness and then to

Accuse the target of inhumanity
And all the attention of the public
Seizes on the accusation and the
Villainous character of the supposed

Malefactor — and the cunning and motives
Of the accuser are overlooked in the
Defamation of the target — and the
Combustion of emotion is useful

To cover up the probability that
The accuser fabricated the charge.

The accusation is
a magician's trick
turning attention
from the accuser's
bad intentions.

Those who would influence the thinking of
Millions of people understand that it's
Advantageous to begin with children
In the schools and to indoctrinate through

Graduation and those with the urge to
Control opinion have utilized the
Media and the screens of computers
And phones and tablets and televisions

And radio waves are broadcasting the
Bitterness of accusation either
Explicitly or implicitly and
Directly or anonymously and

Mixed with accidents and tragedies the
News is a dispiriting bombardment.

Controversy
accusation
hypnotize
lonely
fearful
people.

The radiation of sunlight that the
Earth is absorbing that is providing
The breath of life to each living being
And to each living being that has lived

And died anywhere in the cosmos that
We are aware of is only a small
Proportion of all the light that the sun
Produces as most of the energy

Radiates into space and mixes with
The trillions and trillions and trillions of
Other stars that are circling black holes
And I choose to believe the mystery

Of life and consciousness is beautiful
Even as life is so precarious.

There is no
explanation for
how the inorganic
became organic and how
beings became conscious.

Herbert London

Words of remembrance on the passing of
A friend are surprising gifts that we give
Each other and I knew Herbert as a
Writer in New York City and could not

Have known a lot about him and the list
Of his accomplishments was welcome but
It took a day for a story to emerge
From the bulk of information and to

Resonate that Herbert was scoring at
A pace surpassing his high school and league
Record when the basketball coach removed
Him and Herbert was outraged for many

Years until he absorbed the lesson of
Humility the coach had given him.

I learned
accomplishment
was founded upon
humility.

The river keeps flowing in the winter
Under three feet of ice on the surface
And water is moving consistently
And doesn't dawdle and doesn't hurry

And snow falling in the hollows and on
The limestone bluffs of the river valley
And on the streets and the homes of the town
Of Stillwater is snow for a season

But eventually the snow becomes
The river and then the river becomes
The ocean and then the ocean becomes
The clouds collecting and dispersing in

The sky until eventually the
Water drops and touches the earth again.

As I am drinking
water I am absorbing
the clouds the rain the
snow and the ice the river
and every ocean.

The sun is a balance of gravity
And nuclear fusion persisting for
Billions of years and it radiates in
Every direction and the proportion

Of its energy that warms the earth is
Minuscule — and compared with the trillions
And trillions of other stars it is an
Ordinary phenomenon from an

Analytical viewpoint — but given
The earth's orbit around the sun and the
Rotation of the earth on its axis
And the propitious distance of the

Earth from the sun the right formula of
Ingredients are here to foster life.

There are deserts and
tropical jungles and the
arctic poles and the
oceans and the prairies and
today today and today.

My life arises with my thoughts and I
Bestow proximity and context and
I choose which is magnificent and which
Is insignificant and with the choice

Of magnification I make desire
And repulsion and for me nothing does
Exist outside my awareness of it —
My consciousness is like a fire that lights

The distant cosmos — but when I have
My doubts I am a candle burning in
Darkness — and even with incandescence
There are shadows bordering my thinking —

I practice carefully to remember
There are consequences in my choices.

I am a sun
emanating
into mystery.

The Buddhists believe in the three poisons
Of greed anger and ignorance and we
Consider ignorance to be the source
Of much unnecessary suffering

And ignorance is more productive of
Harm than the most calculating anger
Because the ground of ignorance allows
For the arousal of anger and I

Appreciate that Buddhists don't condemn
Anyone and I am curious and
Am willing to practice every day to
Discover what I am ignorant of

And with my emotional waywardness
I will compose myself within patience.

There is
agitation
and
composure —
earth
and
heaven.

I suppose it happens given the fact
Of birth that there is a choice to be made
Given the never ending sequence of
Events and the fact that so much more than

Can be comprehended is happening
All at this moment here and extending
From here to infinity that the choice
Must be made whether I do believe that

An underlying order pervades the
Cosmos or that the cosmos is governed
By randomality and there is no
Point to compassion and benevolence

Beyond the gratification of me
And I might as well be a mosquito.

I decide without
giving the choice
much thought but
decide with huge
consequence.

I saw three crows in an oak tree on the
Way to my office when I glanced up and
Noticed a crow bobbing on a branch with
Its wings extended as it alighted

On the branch and I saw the other crows
Hopping and turning and then I drove on
Compelled by the chores I needed to do
But I wondered what the street and my car

Would look like from their perch in the oak —
And I questioned whether they have better
Eyes than I do — and could they be hungry —
And is one of them dominant — and the

Crows in a tree on an overcast day
Diverted me from useless obsession.

I was turning and
hopping in my head over
critical words
aimed at a fundraising
letter I had written.

I noticed a gathering of wax wings
In an apple tree and they were chirping
Excitedly together and being
A busybody I approached them and

Then they became quiet — I walked away
And they resumed chirping — and I returned
And they became quiet again while a
Few began protesting what could have been

Suspicion and irritation with my
Unwanted presence — and I remember
The many times I see various kinds
Of birds flying together and turning

Together in the same direction and —
Is it possible they are of one mind?

Perhaps together
they are the spirit
of a gossip
reincarnated
into wax wings.

A chickadee is in the bush outside
My window and others are flying to
The trees in the back yard and a layer
Of clouds is gradually moving and

The furnace is coming on to raise the
Temperature to a setting and then
It's quiet and perhaps my friend Jason
Is climbing the hundred cement steps in

Downtown Stillwater for the exercise
He enjoys and Steve could be attending
To the grandchildren he loves and there is
A girl somewhere I was entangled with

But it's a liberation for me not
To care where she is and what she's doing.

A black hole is
consuming a star
somewhere
but I am
quiet enough.

The tiny flakes of snow are descending
In a curving and meandering way
With enough accumulation over
The night for the thinnest layer of white

To be visible on the roofs of homes
And the barely noticeable snow that
Will not amount to much is giving the
Frigid air a texture under a gray

Sky and the diminished quality of the
Morning light is turning all the naked
Trees the same shade of a drab brown mixing
With the subdued greens of the pines and shrubs

And it's a pleasure for me to let these
Ordinary details envelope me.

The falling snow vanished —
the sky is gray but
the rim along the
far horizon is white.

That I was on the high school wrestling
Team forty-four years ago is a shock
To realize because I do not see
Myself as completely grown even though

I lived in Japan for nine years and was
Married for twenty-seven years and then
Divorced and both my kids are beyond the
Age of twenty-five-years-old and now I'm

Working in the home I grew up in and
Clearing the same driveway of snow that I
Cleared in high school and facing another
Winter and it seems like yesterday that

There were apple blossoms and lilacs and
The leaves were soaking in sunlight again.

Sometimes the
past seems like
yesterday and I
don't remember
what I've forgotten.

Wrestlers were expected to make weight
By late afternoon every Friday in
Preparation for a contest in the
Evening so the entirety of my

Week was aimed at stripping down naked and
Stepping on a scale and proving that I
Was one hundred and five pounds and on the
Preceding three days the morsels eaten

Only reminded me of how much I
Couldn't eat even with the leaning and
Lunging and lifting and leveraging
With all my might for six day of the week

And with my sweating in practice I was
Calculating how many pounds were off.

There were two hours
before the match reserved
for gorging and on
Saturday and Sunday
I discarded discipline.

I emerge from the earth as a fountain
Of thought and emotion and arising
With expression I flow in the creeks — and
Over rocks I am musical in the woods

And in an irresistible current
I roar between the boulders rapidly
And plunge into emptiness silently
And I gather with renewed strength onward

And in my broadness I carry the earth
In shades of brown and green and turquoise and
While moving with great force I am quiet
But my surface undulates ceaselessly —

I merge into oceans and atomize
Into clouds and drop again to the earth.

It's difficult
to surrender
identity and
direction and to
just flow.

Ice is forming on the river and the
Falling snow is turning the river white
And the open water in places looks
Dark and deadly — but I remember last

Summer the river was undulating
And sparkling under the summer sun
And I saw the swallows flitting along
The bank and over the river — and I

Remember a winter in Galveston
Watching the heavy grayness of the sky
And the white cresting waves of Galveston
Bay and I recall the seagulls wheeling

And wailing as I was pedaling my
Bike with the wind along the seawall.

Fluid
memory
arises in
glimpses.

I am a drop of consciousness playing
With words and my consciousness is like the
Blue of the sky today but the sky is
Much more than its blue appearance today

The sky also includes the rain and snow
And the thunder and lightning and
The wind that tears the leaves from the trees
In autumn — and the sky is also a

Part of the earthly circulation of
Rivers and oceans — and the sky transmits
The radiation of the sun — just as
I encompass loneliness and love and

Everything that did and could occur and
Everyone I did and could encounter.

I can't remember
everyone I've met
and can't account for
the traces of them that
live on in me.

I notice birds flying between the trees
Too far to see what types of birds they are —
I watch the sun rising and know it's the
Same sun that the Egyptians idolized —

I enjoy conversation with my friends
Because they tell me about their insights
And their maneuverings and I express
Myself and together we always laugh —

I believe we are spirits cycling
Through lifetimes on the earth and I return
To a mirror and see the face that I'm
Accustomed to and notice the wrinkles

About my eyes and I wonder with what
Other faces I have expressed my lives.

Does my original face
have features I am
accustomed to or does
it resemble
the sky?

I am practically minded and wear
The clothes the seasons demands — even though
I like to appear flamboyantly trim —
And in the winter I'm a blue jeans and

Polar fleece kind of guy who likes pockets
For carrying things as I am geared for
Getting things done — and as winter drags on
My boots become spattered with the salt that

The road crews use to melt the ice on the
Streets and it's a hassle to take off the
Boots and put on my shoes when entering
The house but I do it because it's not

Appropriate to tramp the snow and salt
Inside the house because I'm civilized.

In the winter
it's hard to keep
the weather from
intruding inside.

I know how to tap with my fingers and
Words appear on a screen in front of me
And if I get the first line correctly
The seed inside of the words will blossom —

I don't know when beginning what's inside
That needs getting out and in the middle
I don't know what the ending will be but
There is pleasure and satisfaction in

Balancing cadence grammar and meaning —
There is joy in selecting the words that
Carry impetus and intensity
Without wasting a single syllable

But at the end without a worthy point
The whole poem turns out to be a dud.

With effort and
consistency things
fit together and
I enjoy sharing
with people.

What is the red of the cardinal for?
What purpose does the scarlet serve beyond
The attraction of its mate? Does it live
Only for itself and its progeny?

Because I remember from my childhood
Taking such joy from the sight of the bird
As if its brilliant color transformed the
Drab gray skies the bare branches and the snow

On the ground into an enchanted land —
I would as well ask what is the winter
Solstice for that marks the passing of the
Longest nights and the turning to brighter

Days even though there are many dark days
Ahead when only the cardinal shines.

Childhood joy
and wonderment
from the sight of a
cardinal in winter is
unexplainable.

As a light snow is descending I am
Thinking about cherry blossoms and the
Tradition of writing about cherry
Blossoms in celebration of their blooms

And it is difficult to find something
Fresh to say about the blossoms because
So much has already been said over
The hundreds of years — but when the ground is

Frozen and the trees are sleeping and the
Wind is penetrating cherry petals
Are a vision of delicacy and
A reminder everything is moving

To a timely expression of essence
And beauty does appear persistently.

Cherry blossoms come
when the earth absorbs
the rain and the sun
returns to prominence.

More than in the middle of the summer
Trees express individuality
In the winter when the concealing leaves
Are absent and their forms are visible

And I can see every crook and curve — and
There are the evergreen trees and the shrubs
And as I'm driving about I can see
The differences between the maples

Elms and the oaks but each tree has its own
Way of reaching the sun — and I've noticed
Their common drab brown but today I see
That this one has dignity and that one

Is disheveled and this cottonwood is
Thin while another was struck by lightning.

The trees are a
quiet presence but
with winter wind
they resonate with
motion.

The story of Christ didn't begin in
Bethlehem where a baby was born in
A stable to parents of humble means
In a country strewn with rocks and sand and

Where the Roman Empire was the latest
Victor in a succession of trials of
A people — there was the prophesy and
Yearning for a savior in the midst of

Hardship and emptiness — and the people
Wanted a Messiah and they waited
Patiently while burdened with sorrows and
They needed a gentle master who would

Reveal the meaning of their suffering
And who could summon the strength within them.

The joy of the
Annunciation
and the birth
of the Christ
is fresh today.

It's a fear of mine and maybe yours too —
To be thrown away by people I love
When they know me better than anyone
Does and they are familiar with who I

Am — and there are memories of all the
Fun and I recall the Christmas morning
When I was given to Pamela and
She squealed with joy and had to be with me

For all of a glorious winter — but
The years have passed and Pamela gives her
Attention to her phone and no one looks
At me except to shuck me here and there

And it was not my fault that the cat has
Peed on me — and they really could wash me.

Here I am
Mr. Teddy Bear
on the trash container
by the street
being dumped.

The snow in the night was expected in
My neighborhood but the temperature
Rose through the early hours and by dawn
The snow was slush and difficult to move

But the several inches had to be moved
Because eventually watery
Snow will freeze and adhere to the driveway
As a gnarly hazard — the snow blower

Clogged so I kept my legs moving and scraped
With the shovel as if I were a plow
Clearing the street and when I was finished
Water was flowing on the street — and it

Rained all day and into the next night and
Just before dawn a cold front had arrived.

I can muster my
best efforts but
sometimes a
coating of ice is
unavoidable.

On the occasion of New Year's Day in
Minnesota the trees are dormant and
Their roots are embedded in the frozen
Earth and their branches extending to their

Twigs are motionless under a gray sky
And for them the winter days and months are
Meaningless but for me they are symbols
Of a rhythm of a lifetime in a

Season of bareness — and what a weight the
Stories I remember about my past
Are — and my memories are like roots and
They would be able to hold me firmly

In place if I weren't aware the past is
Gone and I can grow into the future.

The nurturing sun
radiates a life giving
rhythm of seasons
and I choose to believe in
open possibilities.

There are so many choices to make in
The hours of a day and although I
Am often awake — and go to sleep
At the same time — and I rely on a

Predictable schedule — and I know
With good probability where I will
Be and what I will be doing at a
Certain time of day — there is always the

Possibility I could stop and drop
What I am doing — and perhaps that's what's
Meant by being spontaneous — that I
Could do something that I've never done before —

There are so many choices in a day
And dissatisfaction can be helpful.

It takes a little
pain to be poised
and be creative enough
to exploit a
possibility.

Google and Facebook

Somehow Google engineers have harnessed
All the data on the Internet — and
So many people use the Internet
For business and for pleasure and because

Google controls the access to so much
Information Google is powerful —
If I want to know who Svengali was
Or where the nearest Chinese restaurant is

I can type a question and Google will
Inform me — and when I want directions
For driving somewhere Google Maps directs
Me with satellites orbiting the earth —

Google appears to be an all-knowing
Helper who is always available.

The phone I carry
in a pocket with
Google apps is like
a genie who gratifies
unlimited desires.

It doesn't matter what the intentions
Of the Google executives are or
Whether their denials are genuine
Or that they are merely a business and

Lack the power of a government — it
Is true many Google apps embedded
Within the phones that people carry are
Recording where people are going and

What they are doing — and it is true in
Order to gain access to a vast and
Lucrative market the Google big shots
Are willing to magnify the power

Of the Chinese government to observe
Every keystroke the Chinese people make.

The technology
of enveloping
inescapable
surveillance is
being refined.

There was a news report yesterday that
Revealed Facebook has been sharing the
Private messages of its users with
Google and other panjandrums of the

Internet making me nervous that my
Expressions of myself are rippling
Into algorithms manifesting
Into categories established by

Businesses who want to sell me stuff — and
Becoming a data point for profit
Doesn't bother me that much as long as
The offerings are something I might like

But the interpenetration of our
Humanity is becoming scary.

Electronics
and my keystrokes
are revealing my
personality to
to strangers.

There is visibility but also
Remoteness on Facebook that appears to
Make people anywhere touchable and
I am in the habit of exploring

The world and I love the videos of
Elephants and lions and eagles and
I enjoy the acrobatics people
Do and it's easy to forget that I'm

Separated from people and absorbed
In a pixilated screen and as I
Am selecting which postings that I like
The system is providing more of what

I like almost as if I were in an
Animated friendly conversation.

Is Facebook an
electronic
pixilated
opium den?

I play with words and the inspiration
That comes brings energy that carries me
Through the day — and I post my poems on
Facebook sharing my enthusiasm

And I aim for discernment and humor
Filtering my perceptions into as
Few words as possible so that each word
Carries more impact than it normally

Does — and I am mixing the better part
Of my consciousness into the vast and
Intimidating darkness of cyber
Space and my postings are like pebbles that

I'm tossing into a ceaseless ocean
Of swelling and rolling and thundering.

I do my best and
don't worry about
consequences — being
a particle and
a wave.

It's a worthy practice to open my
Perceptions to whatever comes my way
But I select my daily momentum
And with every step I am burdened

With the habits and stories I use to
Explain my experience to myself —
And it is a worthy ambition to
Leave behind as much of me as I can —

And I aspire to comprehend the
Impact of the endless and the boundless
Manifestation of this instant now —
Because before now things were different

And after now things will never be the
Same — and I don't want to use a filter.

I lose myself
with videos
of places I
will never be
on Facebook.

The tallest waterfall on the earth was
Found by a frustrated Jimmy Angel
After his puny plane got stuck in the
Mud on Tabletop Mountain and maybe

He was awestruck by the water plunging
The three thousand feet into a canyon
To be named Devil's Canyon but he walked
For eleven days in the jungle of

Venezuela before he was rescued
And he didn't find the gold he wanted
But the falls were named the Angel Falls for
Him — and I learned of the Angel Falls by

Watching a video on Facebook which
Is not being there but almost as good.

When the water
is plunging into
empty space
is it silent or
does it sound?

Lacking
wisdom and
discretion where
will Google and
Facebook lead us?

Aslan

I love the morning because Aslan the
Mighty created the morning with a
Deep and triumphant voice and as he was
Singing the sound reverberated from

Every direction and with the singing
The stars the moon and the earth appeared and
There was a fresh wind and a light on the
Horizon and hills became visible and

The sky was becoming white and pink and
Gold and Aslan's voice was rising shaking
The air swelling to crescendo and
Summoning compelling impetus and

The first sun rose revealing a valley
With a broad river flowing to the east.

Aslan the lion
shaggy and immense
was facing the sun.

There were mountains in the south and smaller
Hills in the north and the land was raw and
Empty and as Aslan was pacing and
Lilting his song was rippling away

Over the earth and as he was pacing
The valley was greening with grass and the
Grass was moving up the hills like a wave
And the grass was cresting on the mountain

Slopes and the valley was becoming dark
With heather — and bristles with spiky limbs
Were reaching to the sky and sprouting dots
Of leaves — and with a prolonged series of

Notes there were willows along the river
And willow leaves were flowing in the wind.

The branches of a
fully grown beech were
swaying in a breeze
and rhododendron and
wild roses were blooming.

In creation Narnia was bursting
With growth and Narnia was peopled with
Fauns and satyrs and naiads and centaurs
And talking trees and animals and the

Beavers were industrious and the dogs
Were exuberant and all the beings
With the gift of speech were also gifted
With innocence but coincident with

The birthing of life was the intrusion
Of a witch who introduced evil to
The land after she was released from a
Spell when a human boy named Digory

In another world on the verge of doom
Was taken with a moment's temptation.

Curiosity
led Digory to
ring a bell inside
a ruined castle
and release Jadis.

Aslan was aware of Jadis because
Aslan is maker and master — and he
Knew that Jadis was responsible for
The deaths of everyone in the kingdom

Of Charn and that Jadis would dominate
Narnia in the future — and Aslan
Knew what Digory had done and saw that
Digory was lured into a journey

Between worlds by an uncle who was too
Cowardly to go while Digory's Mom
Was dying in bed and his Dad was in
India — and compassion and justice

Were evident even as Aslan was
Lighting the stars and raising the first sun.

Aslan touched noses
with the beasts and the touching
created talking
elephants and antelope
beavers giraffes and horses.

Jadis escaped while Aslan was busy
With Narnia and after Aslan gave the
The gift of speech to a selection of
Animals Digory found his courage

And asked Aslan to heal his mother and
Digory was surprised that Aslan was
Crying with tears of grief for Digory's
Mother but Aslan said since Digory

Had played a part in bringing evil to
Narnia Digory must do a task to
To mitigate the harm — it's curious
That Aslan the mighty would ask a boy

To answer for his human frailty
When Aslan could have done the task himself.

Digory was to
ride a flying horse over
the western mountains
to a garden and pick an
apple from the tree of life.

A wall surrounded the garden and an
Inscription was on the gate warning that
The garden may be entered only by
The gate and the fruit be taken only

For others or forborne and otherwise
A thief would grasp his heart's desire and
Despair and Digory felt the truth of
The words and entered by the gate and he

Took a silver apple as Aslan asked —
To be given to Aslan — and he looked
At the apple and smelled it and a thirst
Came over him and he thought who would know

If he ate one and took another and
With effort he put it in his pocket.

Jadis was inside
the wall and her mouth
was stained with juice and
she was arrogant
even triumphant.

It was the apple of youth from the tree
Of life and Jadis asked why retrieve it
For the lion for the lion to eat
When Digory could taste it and be young

Forever and together they could be
King and Queen of Narnia — or he could
Return to London to his mother and
Could slice the apple into pieces and

Could see his mother's color return as
She ate and she would sleep with healing and
Wake refreshed — and what had the lion done
For him that he should be the lion's slave —

And what would his mother think if she knew
That he could have saved her but he wouldn't?

"Look what the lion
has done — he has made
you as heartless and
as cruel as he is."

"And what business do you have in this world
And what could that beast of a lion do
To you when you return to your own world?"
Asked Jadis but Digory remembered

His mother and knew that she would want him
To honor his promise and there was a
Meanness palpable in the witch's words
That determined his choice and Digory

Abandoned the witch but carried doubt and
Sorrow with him flying east on the horse
Over the mountains and wooded hills and
Past the cliffs and waterfall and evening

Shadow was falling on the plains as he
Took courage remembering Aslan's tears.

The flying horse landed
And nymphs and fauns
parted as Digory
approached and gave
the apple to Aslan.

With a pervasive voice Aslan exclaimed
"Well done!" and everyone in Narnia
Heard him — and Aslan asked Digory to
Throw the apple and seed the soil with its

Magic — and a tree grew as swiftly as
A flag rises and its branches cast a
Light and a wholesome fragrance arose and
Silver apples appeared like the stars and

Aslan asked the Narnians to guard the
Tree as a shield against Jadis because
She would become quite formidable but
The tree would repel her for hundreds of

Years — Jadis seized an apple for herself
And was careless of the consequences.

With no ending of
strength and life
misery will persist
forever.

"Because the magic works according to
Its nature a stolen apple would have
Healed your mother and would have given her
An endless and unhappy life that both

Of you would have regretted but now take
An apple from the tree — and though it will
Not bestow eternal life in your world
It will heal her — and destroy the magic

Rings your uncle used — you do not need them
When I am with you" said Aslan and he
Shook his mane and Digory was floating
In a sea of tossing gold — and sweetness

And power rolled about him and he felt
So happy wise and good — and quite awake.

Digory peeled the
apple of youth and
his mother ate it
piece by piece and
then she slept.

Clive Staples Lewis was an officer
In the British army who survived the
Brutality of World War One as a
Bitter atheist but while he was a

Don teaching literature at Oxford
University he converted to
Christianity and he developed
A facility for writing stories

For children to pass on the faith that was
Inspiring him and he created
Aslan the benevolent and the wise
Lion and Aslan with masterful love

Composed the elements into order
And the kingdom of Narnia appeared.

Every morning is
pristine with the first light of
the sun spreading
over the country even
on a cloudy winter day.

Appearances

I desire to present myself as a
Vision of trimness and in the light of
The afternoon I see how well I did
Shaving in the morning by looking in

The mirror attached to back side of
The sun visor flap while I am sitting
Behind the steering wheel of my car and
I often find the persistency of

The hair on my chin and under my nose
Disturbingly visible but what is
Quite distressing is the obstinacy
Of the hair along the insides of my

Nostrils and just under my nose where it's
Difficult to maneuver the razor.

Every day
I angle in the
corner of my clipper
with its sharp little teeth
buzzing excitedly.

The preliminaries take place as soon
As I leave the shower as a steaming
Pink something and I make sure the right leg
Goes in the right hole of my shorts and that

The shorts are forward to back so that my
Appurtenance is snug and then I note
The label of the t-shirt because it
Needs to be front to back and the pulling

On and taking off and then pulling on
Again is frustrating if I'm wrong the
First time and the label shows me the back
Side and then comes the pulling buckling

And zipping of my jeans and I apply
Deodorant and cologne to be me.

Going through the day
with my t-shirt on
backwards would be like
pushing against the
wind every minute.

I like to squeeze as much as possible
Of the toothpaste out of the tube because
I'm the kind of guy who pretends that he
Doesn't waste anything — although I do

Spend money impulsively so maybe
My toothpaste etiquette serves as a salve
For a guilty conscience — and when most of
The paste has been extruded I like to

Pinch the end of tube with my fingers
Across the seam and I squeeze the tube to
Absolute flatness and roll it up for
Day after day squeezing and rolling with

Joy until I reach the rigid round top
Where it's hard to get the last of the paste.

It is a
reliable
revelation
how long
I delay the
inevitable.

The most dignified personage has to
Pull on his socks and perhaps it is true
He is not aware of the dosage of
Humble pie he is digesting but in

The act he is just an ordinary
Guy — and I had forgotten the pranks I
Pulled in high school until a happenstance
Discussion with a friend reminded me

I used to wear different color socks
And when brave I wore blue and white to gauge
The depth of attention in passing and
Sometimes I would be subtle with green and

Brown and on other days almost normal
With the lightest and darkest shades of blue.

Popularity
escaped me and
I thought nobody
noticed but obviously
I was wrong.

Perhaps the makers of round shoelaces
Are as ignorant and incurious
As their product suggests that they may be
Or perhaps they are just laughing at us

Because the round laces of every pair
Of boots I have ever owned come undone
At least a half dozen times a day — and
I have the indignity of bending

Over in public and tying a lace
Again knowing it will stay tied only
Temporarily — and I must weigh the
Frustration and the embarrassment with

The inconvenience of departing from
My routine and tramping to a shoe store.

There is the
satisfaction of
ripping the laces out
and tossing them
in a trash can.

Minnesota winters are cruel to the
Appendages as the moisture in the
Air vanishes and I awake to the
Painful cracking of my finger tips and

Of my lips and once cracked there's the lengthy
Healing to endure so I prepare while
Getting dressed with lotion on my hands and
Balm on my lips and when leaving home I'm

Wrapped like an eggroll in a polar fleece
And in a jacket with a hood for the
Coldest days that protects my ears and with
Mittens for my fingers — and my toes are

Swaddled within knitted socks and arctic
Boots — and only my nose remains exposed.

My nose is the
foremost part of me
and it has to be
very cold to breathe
with frozen nostrils.

Not every winter day requires the
Complete rigmarole of protection
And on the milder days I engage a
Sense of peacock flamboyance and I may

Choose among an array hats and leave
My ears hanging out and I could select
A brimmed wool fedora imitating
Fred Astaire or I could don my salmon

Proud militant hat from Afghanistan
Looking like two pancakes but normally
I choose between my French berets because
They project a careless jaunty image

And I may pull the floppy hat leftward
Or rightward or backwards as it suits me.

Often I do meld
with the bare trees with my
tan brown black berets
but sometimes I flaunt myself
with blue and green and burgundy.

When snow is
descending constantly
in tiny flakes and
accumulating quickly
everything is covered.

— *Tekkan*

Everyday Mind X

A thaw melted
almost all the snow
except for the piles
the city plows left
along the streets.

The wind chill is way below zero and
I'm walking to my car without mittens
After talking inside a warm room with
My friends — and a friend and I are blabbing

About the supposition that there was
No time or space before the big bang that
Created the cosmos and one pundit
Says because there was no place to stand and

No time to allow it therefore God can
Not exist and there is no afterlife —
And we are strolling outside and the bones
Of my hands are cold as I'm saying just

Because the supposition may be true
Depressing conclusions need not follow.

With freezing hands
there's no time to stand
in the cold and to ponder
indeterminate
facts.

There are days that begin with trouble and
The missteps continue like on Tuesday when
I found the cat vomit by the toilet
And cat poop on the carpet — and being

Harassed by the ringing phone only to
Listen to recorded messages of
No interest to me — and encountering
Error after error in essays that

Require exacting correction while
Needing to finish quickly — and driving
Across town in haste but following a
Succession of the ambling elderly —

It seems I'm fighting a persisting wind
And each movement is testing my patience.

Calm attentiveness
gives way and my
hands express the
jitters.

I light the candle in the chapel that
Serves as our Zendo and we remove the
Extra chairs and carry and place the mats
And the cushions upon which we will sit

And the various bells are arranged in
Position — and before we begin there
Is conversation in the vestibule
And on some mornings I am a part of

The conversation and at other times
I am apart from the group listening
But not conversing — being one of the
Group being shaped by them and shaping them

By the expression of myself is why
My practice is so unpredictable.

Tension between
cooperation
separation
meditation
is a practice.

After a lifetime of cardio and
Weightlifting exercise probably I
Will live to be a hundred years old but
I am not sure that's entirely good

Because I could outlive all of my friends
And I haven't got as much money in
The bank as the retirement gurus
On T.V. say is necessary and

Who will pal around with a forgetful
And deaf and wrinkled old fart even if
He uses one hundred pound dumbbells at
The gym — and I think my kids don't like me —

Negative thinking is very easy —
I have to exercise positivity.

I am asking a
wood-working friend
to make a plaque
that says —
"It won't happen like that."

The cold returned to the valley and the
Ice on the river is deepening and
The air is biting the cheeks of my face
And the cold is sticking to folds of my

Jeans and my walking is painful but I'm
Grateful I can see the blue of the sky
And the impotent sun — and imagine
Being a catfish in the river with

The ice impeding the rays of the sun —
And the enveloping darkness and the
Impossibility of escaping
With the cold passing though its mouth and its

Gills — how could there be an expression of
Personality in the fish's eyes —

With the dull
harmony
of the cold
and the gloom?

Entropy is a scientific word
That means that systems consisting of
Organization and energy will
Over time break down and expire and

The effects of entropy are seen in
The eventual demise of the sun
And in the expansion and cooling of
The galaxies — and even the black holes

Where time does not exist are subject to
Entropy and they will also dissolve —
And I am grateful for the scientists
Who have extended the horizons of

Knowledge but they don't do much — while knowing
We will die — to show us how to live.

Scientists expend
energy learning
how things work but
meaning is an
afterthought.

I was driving east in Bayport towards the
River as I've done thousands of times in
Thirty years — down the hill to the corner
Of Main Street — and today I remembered

The first few days after my family
Moved our home from Hutchinson Kansas where
The land is as flat as a tabletop
To Bayport Minnesota that has hills —

And I recalled the thrill my brother and
I had coasting our bicycles down the
Hill with the wind in our faces and hair
When the little slope seemed like a mountain

Very hard to pedal up to the top
But such a joy to descend so quickly.

I wish it were
still possible to
be so easily
inspired with
simple novelty.

Considering rush hour traffic I
Left an hour before my appointment
So I didn't mind stopping at traffic
Lights but then I was surprised that the stop

And go traffic began so far from my
Destination and I saw the constant
Stream of cars on the ramps feeding into
The highway and I let a cargo truck

With a greasy rear end into the lane
Before me obscuring my view and I
Began to sweat the minutes with each ramp
Feeding more cars in front of me while I

Knew how far there was to go and we crawled
To a stop within sight of my exit.

There were slower cars
in front of me all the way
to the parking lot
and I was a minute late
but I came on the wrong day.

How differently experience appears
From day to day when sometimes my thoughts and
Words are joyous in conversation with
A friend and then at other times I can't

Seem to bridge a gap between us — and I
Know how good it is to spark a thought in
A companion and together we can
Build momentum and enthusiasm

And we can compare perspectives and the
Banter and the laughter are healing and
Clarifying as we give each other
The gift of optimism — but there are

Other days when I become a turtle
And I let the world go on without me.

Lightheartedness
and gratitude
can be practiced
and cultivated.

There is the moment every morning when
I close my eyes and feel my face with
My fingers — as I am using soap and
Washing my face — that is a moment for

Reflection — and it isn't easy to
Step outside and take a good objective
Look at myself — and I discover how
I'm getting along with the people in

My life and where the frictions are and why
I am holding the attitudes that I
Am — and there is the usual thinking
In defense of me that serves to cover

A sense of woundedness that if I'm not
Careful is all that I will ever see.

There are people
I don't want to be with —
but I don't want them
punished or condemned
which is liberating.

A sweeping of snow advances over
The northern plains of America and
On the evening before its arrival
The forecasters are predicting a foot

Of snow followed quickly by a polar
Vortex bringing a degree of cold that
We haven't had for decades — I retrieve
My snowsuit and long underwear and my

Moon boots from storage — assuming that the
Predictions are wrong as they often are —
And it's hard to believe the pattern of
Minimal snow and mild temperatures

Will turn so suddenly so I'll sleep cozy
Waiting for the morning facts to emerge.

One day to another
circumstances are
different so
I'm grateful
the snow blower
works.

Sunlight on a morning when the cold is
Colder than thirty below zero is
As lively as any sunrise can be
And the cloudless sky is as open and

As blue as a mild day in June — but
The cold is bearing down upon the land
And the naked branches of the trees are
Motionless and steam is rising from the

Vents of homes and there is only so much
Words can do in description of the thing
Itself — the cold is an enveloping
Pressure burning and making my breathing

Labored — and when I reenter my home
The emergence of warmth is a relief.

Crows
encounter
cold flying
between
trees.

Now the cold is gone and there will be rain
This afternoon and fog is obscuring
The trees as they look like shadows in the
Mist — as I am leaving in my car I

See the apple trees by the driveway and
There are the innumerable crooked
Twigs and so many drops of water are
Hanging from the crooks — and I can't say that

The sights are beautiful this morning as
The streets are a mess with the melting brown
And salty slush that smears the sides of the
Cars and sticks to my boots but rather I

Would say that there are many glimpses of
Beauty visible any given day.

This is not the
thaw of spring as the
rain will turn to
ice as a cold front
returns tomorrow.

Rain after arctic cold is surprising
And in February there's a bitter
Aftermath as the rain will freeze
And we are left with a coating of ice

On the walkways and driveways and the streets
And for those on the congested highways
Into the city speed is dangerous
And accidents are inevitable —

At my Mom's house the driveway that I have
To clear slopes down to the house and when it's
Icy walking is precarious and
Several inches of snow is forecast so

I will either push a machine and slip
And fall or scrape with a shovel and fall.

Driving out of the garage
and up to the street
I must go fast — or
I'll be spinning my tires
on the icy slope.

When backing out of my driveway after
A day of falling snow I powered through
The fallen snow but got stuck at the road
Where the city plow had left a pile of

Snow — I shoveled once to clear my tires
But could only spin my tires — and I
Shoveled again and then broke out onto
The street and proceeded on my way — it's

Unusual to have a sheet of ice
Under a dumping of snow and when I'm
Clearing my driveway — and my mom's too — I
Could grumble at the circumstances — but

I remember how hard it is to move
Wet heavy snow at the point of melting.

Moving snow is
easier when it's colder
and maybe the snow
atop the ice will
provide leverage?

My Mom's driveway slopes down to the house and
Side by side there are two garages with
A wall to one side so the driveway is
Wide and the snow has to be moved away

From the wall — and the rotational shoot
Of the twenty-year-old snow blower is
Faulty and can only be relied on
To stay put in the forward direction —

So I have to blow across the driveway —
And the with ice under my feet I found
Blowing forward not too hard — but jerking
The machine back with one arm extended

And stepping sideways precariously
Without slipping on the ice was tricky.

It's good to know that
two feet and a snow blower
provide a little
more stability than just
two feet on a sheet of ice.

I moved my car out of my driveway so
That I could snow blow the driveway after
The snow finally stopped falling because
It was getting much colder and the wind

Would be picking up — and afterwards I
Got in the car and attempted a u-
Turn to return the car to the driveway —
But because the city plows hadn't come

The road was a mess and I got stuck and
Another car came along and wouldn't
Pass and waited — and I was flustered and
Bothered and got out to ask the driver

To pass but I was surprised and humbled —
My neighbor wanted to help push me out.

In a moment of
botherment a
hearty young girl
came in the dark
to get me home.

February snow is different from
March snow because the temperature is
Colder and the snow happens to be light
And fluffy in the cold — and I prefer

Moving snow even in the most bitter
Cold to having the snow blower clog with
The heavy melting snow of March because
The snow is hardest to shovel in March —

And the February snow blower at
My Mom's house — even with new spark plugs — is
Different from the November snow blower
Because in November the snow blower

Is frustratingly hard to start but in
February it roars with one hard yank.

I'm sure there are
mechanical reasons
for the difference but
I am clueless.

Writing poems is an oasis in
A day when I may sit at my desk and
Separate myself from being busy
And see if I may find a meaning that

Is worthy of a poem — and today
I am enthusiastic about my
Butter honey nut formula lotion
Even though I'm a manly kind of guy

Because I like the way it smells and how
It sooths my skin during the dry winter
Months — and I am practical and I know
That without the lotion my finger tips

Would crack at odd angles next to my nails
And that is an irritating nuisance.

When the container
is almost empty I will
twist off the end and —
like a Pooh Bear with honey —
finger for every last drop.

My friend returned from a business trip to
India and he remarked about a
Hindu master who while blindfolded could
Read my friend's email address and the phone

Numbers on a business card and my friend
Said that the masters see the world from a
Quantum point of view and some of them use
Their powers for good and some are evil

And I am sure the spiritual life of
India is a deep reality
But in February I do need the
Ability to turn my weariness

Into optimism as the snow is
Falling every day and piling higher.

In India
my friend was asked —
is the snow real?
can you hold a snowflake
in your palm and watch it melt?

A blizzard erases the horizon
And only immediate surroundings
Are visible and it is a proof of the
Power of the sun that even on a

Snowy morning anything can be seen —
I left my car in the garage because
It's likely to get stuck on the streets and
As I am trudging through the snow the fine

Grains of the snow are swirling around the
Wire rims of my glasses and they tickle
Me about my eyes with tiny touches
Of the cold and in order to take my

Short cut I have to climb a bank of the
Compacted snow that a plow left behind.

It is a white world
with a foot of snow cloaking
and bearing down the
branches of coniferous
pines looking so composed.

There will be an end to the snow poems
When the season turns and we are happy
But now we have indistinguishable
Days with grains of snow descending from a

White sky — and there are the daily parades
Of city snow plows slapping another
Pile to the side — and where is vibrancy
When white and shadow predominate — and

It's difficult to remember what I
Did yesterday from the day before or
From what I did last week as the routine
Of snow blower shovel rest repeats and

I suspect there must be something about
Me that enjoys wallowing in the gloom.

Cherry blossoms are
beautiful but
beauty is enhanced
by what comes
before.

A Chautauqua was an American
Gathering of people that was done a
Hundred years ago for entertainment
And story telling and encouragement

With people meeting face to face — but now
We use the Internet and millions of
Americans use Twitter to comment on
The current events — using no more than

Two hundred eighty letters or spaces —
And videos of confrontations will
Rise to prominence inspiring a
Rage with millions of enthusiasts who

Stab their enemies with daggers as they
Hide their identity in cyber space.

Creating
scapegoats is
easier when
guardians are
anonymous.

There is pathology broadcast by the
Mass media — whether in the game shows
Where the adults are reduced to shrieking
Children — in the news reporting on the

Daily violence and tragedies — or
In the political narratives when
Over time the politicians and the
Reporters and the pundits take both sides

Of the same issues and it becomes clear
The issue is not the issue but that
The acquisition and maintenance of
More and more power among a select

And closed group of elites is the issue
And the voters are manipulated.

People are angry
because disturbing
narratives are created to
produce manipulated
angry people.

Humans in masses are scary because
Of our squabbling and scapegoating and
Tribal instincts and tunnel vision — and
We are easily manipulated

And vulnerable to mass hypnosis —
And there are demons among us who are
Driving us like cattle to destruction
Assaulting the American system

Of the separation of powers with
Devilish tricks of demagogy
With such furious ingenuity
Practicing the arts of accusation —

Humans are volatile and dangerous
Capable of unthinking cruelty.

Political ads
broadcasting thirty seconds
of accusation
rely on fear and envy
to channel revenge.

Before words were written on parchment they
Were remembered and passed on by word of
Mouth — if they were important enough — and
Someone said we are what we think and all

That we are arises with our thoughts — with
Our thinking we make the world — and he said —
Speak or act with an impure mind and your
Troubles will follow you like a wheel that

Follows the ox that draws the cart — and he
Said — we are what we think — all that we
Are arises with our thoughts — with our thoughts
We make the world — speak or act with a pure

Mind and happiness will follow you as
Your shadow — and these are remembered words.

This is a saying
of the Buddha
written later
in the Dhammapada.

[Adapted from Thomas Byrom's translation]

Friends are good for showing me other ways
Of living and I know a busy guy
In retirement who enjoys nature
And photography with a window that

Opens to a lake and he has a bird
Feeder in easy sight of the window
And during winter while we are reading
Samples of our writings to each other

There are yellow belly sap suckers and
Nuthatches coming and going and he
Says that if you put up a bird feeder
The birds will come and yes the migrating

Humming birds will return — and who could think
Such delicate birds would be migrating?

Leisure isn't
having nothing to do
but being free
from aggravation —
and loving life.

Once in a while an eagle is skimming
A current of air and if I were a
Photographer with an adjustable
Lens I could bring the bird into focus

And follow its effortless patrolling
For prey and I would be on the hunt for
The capture of the perfect shot in an
Instant with the correct shutter speed and

The necessary quantity of light —
And then I trade places and imagine
The eagle's ability to see and
The terrible gripping power of its

Talons and the ripping use of its beak
And its life of hunger and satiety.

The contrails of a
barely visible jet are a
hint of hundreds
of separate lives moving
rapidly across the sky.

Some people are clever enough to have
Figured out that a million seconds is
Almost twelve days and a billion seconds
Amounts to about thirty-two years and

A trillion seconds is near thirty-two
Thousand years — and the Lascaux cave drawings
In France are seventeen thousand years old —
And to study the events of the Big

Bang scientists will slice a second — and
A million parts are called microseconds
A billion parts are called nanoseconds
And a trillion are called picoseconds —

And in the observable cosmos
Are untold trillions and trillions of stars.

Does any of this
information explain
life and consciousness
or put cruelty and
kindness in context?

It is said that inside a space the size
Of a trillionth of the period at
The end of a sonnet the cosmos popped
As hot as ten thousand trillion trillion

Degrees and for fourteen billion years it has
Been expanding and accelerating —
And the temperature of the cosmos
Now is three degrees and it is thought that

At some point the stars will flicker out and
The black holes will evaporate — and as
Long as there is mass the planets will
Orbit but when the temperature is

Absolute zero the molecules will
Dissolve and the particles dissipate.

Beyond the alpha
and the omega there is
no knowledge possible
but my beating heart
continues.

There was another blizzard yesterday
And I cleared both of the driveways twice
Because it's easier to pace the work
Than to have too much to move at the end

Of the day — and the difficulty is
The compacted pile the city plows leave
Across the entrance of the driveway that
Can only be removed in slices with

The snow blower — and overnight a thin
Layer of fluff descended giving me
A little more to do — with a shovel
I scraped around in a meandering

Pattern curving my path and avoiding
The repetition of the back and forth —

Circling
sashaying like
Napoleon
outwitting the
Austrians
and Russians.

It is true that a life of resentment
Of people and circumstances is a
Wasted life and it is not easy to
Recognize the habit of resenting

As a source of my unhappiness but
Another impending blizzard with the
Forecast temperature rising above
Freezing and therefore bringing sleet and the

Worst of heavy wet snow is presenting
The opportunity for practicing
Acceptance and for elevating snow
In February to the level of

A tragicomedy — and who is to
Blame except for a Doofus Deity.

From the window above
my Mom's driveway it appears
what I thought was a straight line
is more of an angle and
now there is more snow to move.

If there are consciousness particles that
Come from a consciousness field and if such
Particles are waving permeating
Everything that I am able to see

Maybe I should think of myself as a
Node of consciousness with a peculiar
Ability to make choices and to
Evolve or devolve depending on the

Quality of my choices — so when I
Am presented with another falling
Of snow that I have to move with a snow
Blower and shovel I could be fuming

And occupied with the injustice or
I could be shoveling and marveling.

Imagine the result
of thirty years of
unresolved resentments
piled one over
another.

For those of us who don't dress up for an
Office it's routine in winter to wear
Insulated and oversized moon boots
That rise to cover our ankles as the

Conditions in Minnesota are not
Conducive to a ballerina on
Tippy toes in slippers as we get used
To clomping and moving the snow — and we

Get weary in our plodding so I will
Bend enough to untie my boots at the
Top and might even loosen the laces
But it's hard to bend all the way over —

Using my toes as leverage behind
My heels I pull my feet out of my boots.

About the middle of
a snowy February
a what-the-hell
attitude creeps
over us.

The snow blown by a hard persisting wind
Into a drift is different than it was
Before the wind as it gives a crunchy
Reaction when I'm stepping on it — and

The remnants of the blizzards piling one
Over another through the season are
Not the same snows that they were when falling
From the sky as temperature and time

Are having a continuous effect —
As soon as the weather warms and the snow
Melts in the afternoon and freezes in
The evening a crust will emerge on the

Surface and the piles along the street will
Deform as the melting begins to bite.

After twenty years
of clearing the same driveways
with the same tools I
notice I'm not quite the same
collection of attitudes.

The point of meditation is to wake
Which is what we say to each other and
Which implies that there is a boundary
To cross without directions where to go

And now that I've become familiar with
My history and propensities and
Am aware of the chattering antics
Of my thought I want to penetrate my

Life and throw off body and mind and be
Enlightened by myriad things as a
Famous monk remarked centuries ago
But it's also said the desire for

Awakening can become a problem
Leaving a person with nowhere to stand.

I don't really know
how to be nowhere
as I am always
somewhere
thinking.

The Japanese position vermillion
Tori gates at the entrance to their shrines
And the gates are called the abode of birds
Because the birds will perch on them — they are

So simple being only two posts topped
By two beams — and they are said to mark the
Crossing from the mundane to the sacred —
And I have crossed without noticing a

Difference and smirked — but after thirty
Years I remember them and recognize
That every day I may transition from
The ordinary into the sacred

As long as I believe the transcending
Is possible and is worth the seeking.

Another snowfall needs
moving and the snow may be
a tori gate as
I leverage energy
over negativity.

I wouldn't want to live without being
One of a group that delights in meeting
Each other where there is no striving for
Preeminence or authority to

Reduce our companions to a lesser
Status — and in my group we take turns in
Sharing the attention and every one
Turns to face the speaker and the practice

Of listening and responding in turn
Reveals that my concatenation of
Thinking is not unique to me but in
Fact my friends often share my patterns of

Thought — and the differences that emerge
Serve to show the way to innovation.

I heard about grabbing
the rear bumper of a
vehicle and about sliding
while trying to stay standing —
called hookybobbin.

Alcoholics are like pennies with one
Side showing miserable and lonely
Individuals on the way to a
Demise — but on the other side we are

Joyous and free as we learn to break the
Walls of isolation through sincere and
Patient communication — as we learn
To listen more than we did before — now

We rely on something we can't see or
Touch except when it emerges in the
Words of our fellow alcoholics and
The circumstances of our lives — and it

Becomes easier to trust no matter
What happens gratitude is possible.

Resentment
cherished long
enough leads
to my
demise.

To begin the discussion sometimes we
Read from a text — and I have heard the words
A gazillion times — and I like to read
To show off my articulation — and

I don't know if people are listening
Because they have heard the same words also —
But I plow ahead because there are sure
To be a few words that initiate

A conversation — I will be flowing
Pronouncing expertly while I'm thinking
About the snow and having to move it
Or I'm yearning for a lovely movie

Star — as the profundity of the words
And the meaning escapes my attention.

I can always
appear attentive
by expanding on
several ideas
within the text.

As I am dealing with the mess of a
Snowfall and subject to the timing of
The city snowplows I have often thought
About what it's like to be driving such

A forceful machine slapping the snow
To the side no matter how heavy and
Wet the snow may be — as I imagine
Myself a captain of the city streets —

And as a lowly owner of a home I
Am dependent on the plows to finish
With the snowfall and I must wait until
Their final pass that leaves the hardest and

Highest pile of compacted snow that takes
The utmost effort to shove to the side.

I resent the ease
with which they clog
my driveway — and
dislike that they always
get to my street last.

From my office there is a hill at the
Corner where I take a right turn and in
The middle of a blizzard before the
Plows clear the way there is no chance to build

Momentum up the hill and I have to
Judge whether it's possible to ascend
The slippery slope — and I was half way
Up but my tires were spinning without grip —

So I backed to the corner and turned down
A steeper slope towards a much higher hill
But because I picked up enough speed I
Barely made it to the top — and then I

Turned up a little hill without the push
I needed and almost got stuck again.

To get home I need
to guess the viscosity
of compressed snow and
fluffiness is a problem
but there's grip in heavy snow.

At my spot on the earth we have the March
Sun that is bright early in the morning
But the temperature is zero which
Is darn cold for humans — and I know that

Our sun and planets are moving as a
Unit orbiting in the Milky Way —
And I know the Milky Way is also
Moving together as a unit and

Expanding from where the Big bang happened
Along with all the other hundreds of
Billions of galaxies — and though events
Seem to happen gradually on earth

The earth is orbiting in the Milky
Way at five hundred thousand miles per hour.

The blue sky of morning
is concealing so much
of our reality
as I am sitting
quietly in a chair.

It is a bubble of a thought that burst
A moment before its proper time or
You could say it's a hiccup or even
An interruption of a really good

Inspiration that led to something quite
A bit better than itself later on
But as it is doesn't cohere into
A complete package that elicits a

Sense of satisfaction — as it looks like
A compendium of nonsensical
Elements that are fine enough if they
Were separate but together they are

Ridiculous — so I have to remark
Who could imagine the platypus?

And yet it swims
gracefully and waddles
along on land — and lays
its eggs and deploys
venom and growls.

It is a morning unlike the mornings
Of the previous weeks as I sit at
My desk and look out the window at the
Blue sky because today I have to put

On my wide brim hat to shield my eyes from
The emanations of the sun — and I
Enjoy absorbing the sunlight shining
On the piled snow seeing the pin-point jewels

Where the light is refracting into blues
And greens and reds in the snow that is just
Outside my window — and I am weary
Of so many overcast and snowy

Days and now it is a joy that the sun
Is bright enough for me to shield my eyes.

March is the snowiest
month perhaps but
the blooms of tulips
apple blossoms and
roses are coming.

We came to a point where the dry food was
Not healthy anymore as it induced
A urinary blockage in Johnnie
And then Henry got kidney disease and

Needs wet food from now on and it's better
To include Kit in the routine but then
One of them would look at the dish and not
Eat so we mixed two flavors together

And that worked for a while but we needed
Further inducement so a blender is
Useful for making puree with milk or
Water added sometimes but we came to

A point whatever is tried one of them
Looks at the dish turns around and walks off.

I am a chef for
discriminating
felines who don't care
as much as I do
about nutrition.

The trees in winter are in a trance of
Sleeping with their roots well established in
The earth firmly holding in the barren
Season and weathering the howling wind

And in their stark nakedness they become
Almost invisible but they are a
Quiet presence when I notice them in
Sunlight reminding me of my yearning

For roots attaching strengthening myself
Knowing I grow or wither depending
On whether I have the energy and
The will to embrace the supposition

In the midst of the incomprehensible
Suffering there is also a meaning.

There is a call
to awake to the
possibility
of growth in the midst
of difficulty.

The snow has piled storm after storm until
At the end of the driveway the piles are
Higher than me — and when I see the piles
About town I'm prideful about how we

Do manage to push aside enormous amounts
Of snow every year and go about our
Business — with rainy days forecast this week
I wonder whether the season turned and

Whether this is the week the snow begins
Irreversibly to pool on the streets
And flow downhill to the river — even
Though there may be snowy days ahead the

Preponderance of winter is over
And the sun will be reviving the earth.

Regardless of seasons
my hot water heater
provides enveloping
cascading warmth
every morning
shower.

The earth is cloaked in deep layers of snow
And walking between the piles I can feel
The cold emanating from the snow as
A persisting force that necessitates

The wearing of my warmest clothes and for
A thinner guy the cold penetrates and
I've left my neck and hands exposed with the
Intention of feeling the cold because

I am acclimated to the cold and
Even proud to be an inhabitant
Of the desolate northern plains hardy
Enough to be here as it isn't really

The weather that's the difficulty but
My wariness of people is what's hard.

Articulating my
occasional sense
of isolation among
people isn't easy —
the cold is easier.

Michelangelo was fired with a
Conception of God surrounded by his
Angels in heaven reaching out with his
Index finger to touch the finger of

Adam on Earth and perhaps in the act
Of touching God communicated a
Spark of divinity and a freedom
Of choice allowing for a growth into

The humane or for a dissipation
Into evil — and by the Renaissance
In Italy evil was already
Old in the world and people needed their

Consolations and inspirations and
We really aren't much different today.

Did Adam feel like
I did when opening
a tin of cat food
and slicing the tip of
my index finger?

A cloud has descended in Stillwater —
The homes and trees are emerging
Momentarily as I am driving —
Headlights are lighting the mist — the tires

Are splashing in the pools of the water
Collecting in the low places of the
Worn streets — as the accumulation of
Snow has peaked and the melting has begun —

The water is rippling and rushing
Across the many streets of Stillwater —
Down to the river — as the momentum
Of the days are evolving and snow may

Be possible yet — but I am feeling
The boisterous buoyancy coming with spring.

The sun
by itself in
the sky
will have
potency.

It takes practice to be spontaneous
As I am often taken by an urge
To argue a point of politics or
A voluptuous woman appears and

My pulse quickens — I have ammunition
To advance a case and I posses the
Qualities to make a favorable
Impression but it's not so easy to

Seize the moment and a second is just
Enough for hesitation to emerge —
I balance hope and defiance — passion
And carelessness — and just like faith and doubt

Produce good practice — excitement and poise
Can be joyously unpredictable.

Nothing is more
intoxicating
than clarity and
adrenalin.

There is rhythm to a day beginning
Before sunrise and the art of living
Usefully for me is learning how to
Harmonize my energy and relax

And when the sun rises I can see it
Through my window and I welcome the light
As if today were a day of boundless
Possibility and I were a child

But then there are responsibilities
And so many details and events that
Need attention and something will happen
That demands an extemporaneous

Response and I find myself in traffic
And everyone is driving too slowly.

A letter from
the Internal Revenue
Service is threatening
to seize my assets and I
need to see my accountant.

Getting a letter from the I.R.S.
Distorts the rhythm of a day as the
Threatening words are easy to see but
It's perplexing and excruciating

To decipher what the problem is — and
Last year my accountant untangled a
Mistake that the agency made but it
Seems different agents are repeating

The same mistake again — and another
Letter will have to be sent and I will
Have to navigate through their telephone
System and wait for an hour before

I reach an agent to persuade her to
Stop the impending seizure of assets.

While I was waiting
on the phone a
little red squirrel
scampered about the hedge
outside my window.

The melting of the snow progresses at
A gradual pace as there are cooler
And warmer days — and the piles along the
Streets that the city plows have left are the

Last to melt and I see the same houses
And bushes and the trees that are always
There as I'm driving and I am happy
The snow is disappearing as the snow

Is grimy and crusty and there are leaves
And tulips and apple blossoms to look
Forward to and — kerunk — a hole in the
Street jarred my tire and back and dang it

It's easy to daydream while driving and
I really hate hitting potholes in spring.

Dang it
a pothole
what the hell
was I thinking?

It can't be seen by only looking at
A person but once the conversation
Begins and honest words are exchanged then
I can see the battered appearance and

I can sense the depth of sincerity
In the selection of words and in the
Quiet and measured pace of expression
And then I know here is a kind and a

Well meaning person who has suffered and
Has determined to use intelligence
And experience and whatever pride
There might have been is washed away and now

There is a poise and a readiness to
Respond with a wealth of humility.

There is a sweetness
that only arises
from suffering and
a determination
to be helpful.

I was awake yesterday morning at
This time but I went to sleep later than
Usual and today my nose tickles
And there's fluid sloshing in my nasal

Cavities on the verge of eruption
And my eyes are dry and irritated
And I should be enthusiastic and
Energetic by now but instead there

Is the urge to go back to bed and I
Can't go back to bed and need to be as
Productive as possible — and last night
I read the words of a scientist who

Was considering the present moment
Writing it's hard to define what it is.

A squirrel is
climbing the branches
of a maple tree and
I coughed
three times.

A city takes on an identity
By the events that happen within it
And Chicago isn't recognized for
The transparency and honesty of

Its government so I wonder what the
Artist intended in placing The Bean
In a central plaza of the city —
And as a stainless steel sculpture curving

Like a bean it perfectly reflects the
Clouds and the artistic skyscrapers and
The many people who have the leisure
To enjoy it — and perhaps there is no

Cynicism implicit in it and
We are simply meant to savor the clouds.

I should dispense
with cynicism
and enjoy the
simplicity
and beauty.

The sound of the rain falling on the roof
At the beginning of the morning is
Peaceful and it isn't the first shower
Of the season but it is a soaking

Of the earth and a revival of the
Trees and bushes that have been dormant for
The long winter months and the air is damp
And the rain is spattering the puddles

On my driveway and the sky from which the
Drops are falling is misty and perhaps
The water will seep into my basement
And I'm prepared for excess water and

The gentle bombardment of the drops of
Rain will usher in a resurrection.

Each little drop
striking the earth
being absorbed
is one little touch
of revival.

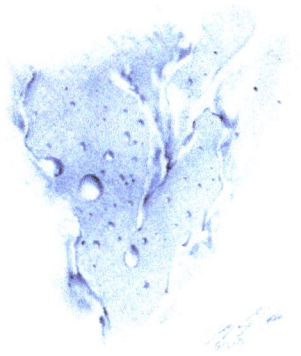

Brown grass and leaves on the ground left over
From fall are revealed on a sunny
Day and the branches are bare and without
The buds that will be coming soon — and the

Few clouds are transparent and are high in
The sky — and the clouds transforming from day
To day are not the things a person would
Notice as they are taken for granted

Like the grass the leaves the sun and the moon —
But the permutations of the earth are
Embedded in me — and as I'm getting
Better at quieting the clamor of

Fearful thoughts I am more likely to see
And rejoice with snowy egrets flying.

The ground is
sodden with
yesterday's
rain and is
preparing
miracles.

Sleep when it comes is a gift as I can
Forget about the troublesome details
Taking up my time and there is the drift
Into slumber and the waking early

In the morning and how well I manage
To sleep depends upon the amount of
Fear I carry in my days and depends
Upon whether I am seeing the things

That are flexible from the things that aren't
And whether I turn my fears over to
An invisible and untouchable
Power and on whether no matter what

Happens and even if I die I do
Believe in waking as if from a dream.

Dozing on my feet
or in my chair in
the afternoon is
what I do when not
managing well.

If I don't get moving in the morning
And don't feed and brush the cats and change the
Water in their dishes then I've giving
My mind the opportunity to think

About how lonely I am and how hard it is
To meet a girl while everyone else seems
To be happy — or I will ruminate
About the difficulties of making

Money — so I have to get up early
And do chores and meet my fellow sober
Alcoholics — and I have to practice
Turning from negativity to the

Positive and as long as I'm talking
With my friends it's easy to be joyous.

I make nonsense
noises or sing when
brushing and feeding
the cats — which
they expect.

I am ensconced in my neighborhood and
Once the piles of snow have vanished from the
Borders of my yard along the street I
Notice the gargantuan heaps in the

Parking lots and when they expire — as
They are on the verge of expiration
Now — I rejoice because the dreary months
Of winter are over but the sky is

Leaden the temperature is freezing
And people are mouthing the word snow and
The trees are moving with a bitter wind
Without their buds and I am questioning

Is today an April morning or a
Twilight resurrection of November?

This is a trick
weathered
Minnesotans
should expect
by now.

I am holding my two thermoses of
Coffee in my mittens while stepping through
A foot of snow on my way from home to
My office — which is what I do when it's

Not a good idea to take the car
From the garage because it's likely to
Get stuck on the street within sight of my
Home — and that would be a nuisance — so I'll

Sit on my chair and drink coffee and look
Out the window at the blowing snow and
At the branches of trees swaying in the
Wind and rejoice that on days like today

We can be within warm homes — and how did
People in the past manage to survive?

From the basement
I retrieved the one
piece snow suit and
the big boots that
almost reach my knees.

The first ever photo of a black hole
That is fifty-five million light years off
Was made by synchronizing atomic
Clocks and by focusing eight radio

Telescopes on several continents — thus
Making the earth a telescope — and by
Waiting for the moment when the weather
Was clear in Spain and Antarctica and

Chile — and the image shows a glowing
Doughnut with the edge nearest to the earth
Appearing brighter than the further side —
And the scientists deduce the burning

Ring is composed of the dust and gas flung
Around the hole and instantly consumed.

The cosmic
sinkhole
trapdoor
collapses
time.

Albert Einstein deduced the existence
Of black holes but before the photo was
Taken today no one had seen them and
To produce the photo astronomers

And physicists and mathematicians
And engineers combined their efforts — an
Algorithm was fashioned to remove
The atmospheric humidity of

The earth — and the scientists say that the
Extremity of the bending of light
Is such that if one sat on the edge of
The event horizon one could see the

Back of one's own head — a curious and
A puzzling statement that's hard to grasp.

With a celestial body
I would like to sit on the
edge of the event
horizon with a cane pole
and fish for mysteries.

If I didn't have to move the snow and
If it weren't so dangerous and messy
To drive about it would be a pleasure
To watch all the little differences

That snow manifests — it is falling in
Fine grains and slanting and curving about
Today and when a grain touches my face
There's a tiny tap of moisture on my

Cheek — and nature doesn't care about my
Temperament and I have to adapt to
Circumstances and it's natural for
A person on the earth to struggle to

Keep body and soul harmonious
While attending to the details of life.

Were the blue skies
and the reviving
landscape days ago
a dream — because today
looks like February.

I have a simple conception of sight
About the ability to see things
That I'm looking at — but the people in
Australia are walking about up side

Down and a scientist says that space is
Composed of interlocking rings that are
Billions and billions of times smaller than
An atom — and a physicist says that

Gravity operates upon mass and
Crushes every large object into a
Sphere and even though Mount Everest seems
Imposing — from an astronomer's view —

The earth would feel as smooth as a cue ball —
If I possessed gargantuan fingers.

What about a
consciousness
embodying this
cosmos and interlocking
cosmoses?

A couple of sparrows are content to
Sit on the branches at the top of the
Maple while the chickadees are diving
And flitting about and hopping in the

Bush outside my window — and the snow on
The bush melted yesterday into a
Dribbling that froze over night into
Such delicate icicles — and drops are

Forming from the icicles this morning
And falling — the chickadees are turning
Their heads and hopping a foot away from
Me in the bush with quick little movements —

The birds aren't bothered by the overcast
Sky or by snow on the ground and the roofs.

The white sky
is glowing
brilliantly
from sunlight.

Do you have those Saturday afternoons
When you don't know what to do with yourself
When the usual routine is to go
To the gym and grocery shopping but

This Saturday you just don't want to go
Because there's the intuition that life
Has so much more to offer but somehow
You've allowed yourself to get pigeonholed —

And the workweek is over and there was
No thought of behaving differently
Until the prospect of pumping iron
Again begets a undeniable

Revulsion making you paralyzed in
The parking lot wondering what to do?

Thank God for
ennui — I'd be
repetitive and
boring without
it.

What made the cat who was destined to be
Named Johnnie attractive to me in the
Animal shelter was his jump onto
My lap — his curling up and his purring —

Fifteen years later his urinary
Tract became infected and from then on
He needs expensive prescription canned food
And he waits to be fed four times a day

And for the last several years my home is
Transformed by the insistent yowling of
Johnnie begging to be fed when I come
In the door or periodically in

The day and he won't be quiet and all
I can do is learn to ignore the noise.

The affectionate cat
re-emerges sometimes
between bouts of
unquenchable
appetite.

Wolfgang Pauli noticed that a minute
Amount of energy was missing from
His equations so he postulated —
And has been proved correct — the existence

Of the neutrino — a subatomic
Particle with zero mass and without
An electric charge — that originates
From the continuing fusion within stars —

And at the speed of light the cosmos is
Penetrated with neutrinos that pass
Through the densest matter including the
Earth and humans with no discernable

Effect and scientists are wondering
Do they oscillate? Are they dark matter?

Which makes me
speculate what else is
penetrating me
constantly?

We would be better off if all of us
Were much more skeptical of what we read
In newspapers because journalism
Breeds cynicism and tribal thinking —

Which doesn't mean that journalists are not
Necessary to free societies —
But journalists cater to the masses
And bitterness and accusation make

Attractive headlines — it is difficult
To erase a negative portrayal
Of a person's reputation once the
News is circulated — and journalists

Escape the scrutiny that they deserve
By directing the attention elsewhere.

Power
and deceit
cooperate
like a hand
in a glove.

It is difficult to believe that each
Of us has a destiny that is an
Appointed destination that we can
Realize only after making the

Necessary decisions — coming as
We do from parents who came from parents
Who each carried stories about themselves —
As the stories are forgotten with the

Passing generations — and who can say
How much depends upon the mixing of
Personalities and dispositions —
As stories never tell the whole story —

Perhaps it's better not to think too much
Or to value — destiny — very much.

Destinies are made
in retrospect by
making connections
that maybe were true
and maybe not.

The trick about writing poetry is
Not to become too enamored of a
Word or a line too early — I don't have
To know what the ending will be and I

Don't have to have clarity from the start —
The playing with words is fun if I am
Willing to throw away what doesn't work
Because I know with practice a meaning

Will emerge and the meaning takes form as
Suitable words come to mind and the run
Of syllables and the mixture of the
Vowels and consonants find harmony

As I am hunting for illustrations
For how the world works — without illusions.

False starts are
frustrating
but patience
finds
satisfaction.

I'll break the rules of poetry with glee
And write a poem without images
Propounding only words and ideas
Raising a windstorm with consonants and

Vowels — and because meaning is vital
To me and is the most elemental
Ingredient of a human life I
Will winnow away the decorous in

Favor of significance — because
The world is like the bare branches with buds
And without a celebration of the
Budding of spring what would be the point of

Living a human life — and I want to be
Resonant like the wind passing in leaves.

I want to
write the right
words in a
proper order without
wasting a syllable.

A week ago the snow returned at a
Seeming tipping point and retarded the
Arrival of spring — but today the ground
Is clear again and the grass is greening

And I was frustrated and the people
I talked to were soured by the turn the
Weather took because it's been a long and
Snowy winter and we yearn for warmth but

The river is free of ice and didn't
Flood the downtown businesses as was feared
And we realize that resplendent days
Are on the way and the couple rainy

Days we had are normal in April and
I really didn't have to shovel the rain.

When the
impending
snowstorm
passed my
mood lightened.

I am leveraging as much morning
Energy as possible to open
My eyes and ears so that I inhabit
My living in cooperation with

The rising sun and what's noticeable
Is the spontaneity of waking
Again with an optimism that makes
Light of my burdens and cherishes the

Freedom to sing nonsense to my cats as
I'm brushing them — and there is no human
Sense in the singing but lightheartedness
And daily renewal carry impact —

I believe my cats know what to expect
And brushing and singing make me happy.

For much of my
living waking again
was a regurgitation
of burdens.

There comes a day every spring when I hear
Birdsong again with the rising sun and
I have no certainty about exactly
On which day the joyful creatures arrived

From their seasonal migration as the
Air is chilly and damp and I keep my
Windows shuttered until the warmth is well
Established — in the morning I hear the

Birds again responding to the sunrise
And marvel that such delicate creatures
Can transition through the air and return
To a familiar location and I

Admire their propensity to see
The sun rising up and to celebrate.

The birds remind
me of the beauty
and the mystery of
the earth beyond
comprehension.

There once was a woman named Jill
Who lived on a prominent hill
She was famous in town
For fooling around
And for making an ass out of Bill.

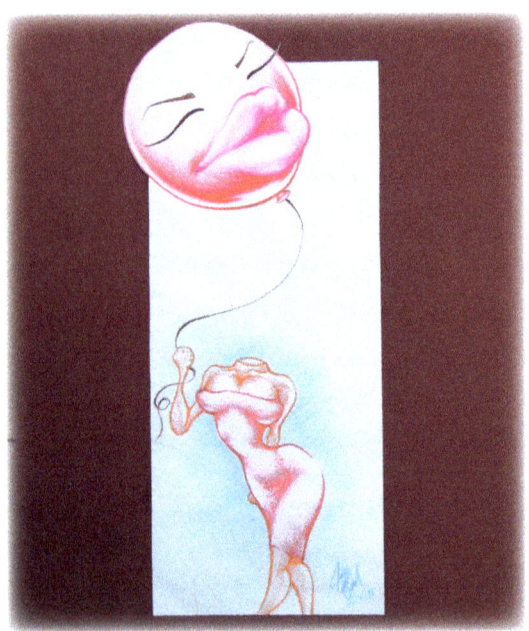

The speaker was passionate about the
Night he was camping above the tree line
In the Sierra Mountains and waking
Under the moonlight and absorbing the

Panorama of the mountains and the
Canyons and feeling the significance
Of his life diminish to nothingness —
And he felt himself dying but then an

Answering response arose that in his
Smallness he is a part of the cosmos
And before and afterwards disappeared
And there was only presence and though the

Experience happened years ago he
Has been transformed ever since that night.

The experience was
unbidden and however
much desired it can't
be gained by
force of will.

I dropped in the beef stew meat and emptied
The cans of stewed tomatoes green beans and
Kernels of corn — and then I cut mushrooms
Cauliflower broccoli and onions

Into appropriate pieces and put
Them into the crock pot — it's curious
To me that very much foodstuff can go
In the slow cooker and yet there is room

For plenty of water — I calculate
The amount of chicken powder needed
Knowing it's easy to add some later
But I'm tempted to use a lot at once —

Last Sunday morning I used too many
Mushrooms and forgot about the onions.

On returning home
outside of my door
of all the ingredients
I smelled green beans
and broccoli.

Transitions

Before the assassinations of the
Kennedy brothers and Martin Luther
King and before the Tet Offensive there
Was the Beatles Revolution and the

Intoxication of rhythm and blues
And the generation older than me —
While I was self-conscious and clumsy and
Awakening to loneliness and desire —

Grabbed me by the balls — and breasts and lips and
Long hair and visions of ecstasy in
San Francisco took me over and I
Listened to music on the radio

And wanted romance and liberation
And I was ashamed of my family.

My Dad the
Congregational
minister once
a month
hacked
my hair
short.

There was a sharp edge to my Dad as he
Condemned so many people and so much
Of popular culture and now I know
That he saw himself as a failure which

Exacerbated the vehemence of
Of his opinions — as he immigrated to
America from Australia as
A youthful Christian minster who loved

Classical music and who aspired
To be scholarly and inspirational
But instead he encountered persisting
Opposition and indifference and

He hungered for appreciation but
Serious ambition is dangerous.

He was a little
fellow in a very large
country and people
were misdirected and he
couldn't change anything.

I remember listening to my Dad
As he was driving and I was sitting
Beside him and he stressed the importance
Of having a philosophy of life

Which meant discovering reasonable
Explanations that can only be done
By absorbing the intelligence of the
Most brilliant people who wrote histories

And philosophies — and to find the truth
Meant sorting through the centuries of thought
And learning to distinguish between that
Which is formidable and diseased

And that which is penetrating and honest —
As only the very best are humane.

His vehemence was
off-putting and as
an introverted
adolescent I
only wanted friends.

I understood my Dad well enough to
Respect his ideals and I admired
His courage and ambition when he quit
The church and established a journal of

Opinion but I also resented
Having to grow up with controversy
And partisanship and I divided
Myself from America by living

In Japan for almost a decade and
By becoming a Buddhist and taking
Up a quest for enlightenment and I
Wholeheartedly believe Americans

Put too much faith in ideology
Even in vicious ideologies.

Today hindered by
worldly attachments
I'm practicing to
dispense with body and
mind and be liberated.

The decades pass quickly and opinions
Are like the clouds that are similar from
Day to day and I practice naming my
Emotions and when I am angry or

Afraid or indulging in self-pity
It becomes easier over time to
Let my emotions go and I can choose
Whether to be unhappy or to see

The miracle of a sunrise on a
Frosty morning or to take note of the
Different manifestations of snow
Or to enjoy the return of robins

And when snow on the ground is melting
The afternoon warmth is marvelous.

I brought a wife and
children from Japan
to live in America
and I began working
with my Dad.

The Buddha began a tradition of
Leaving home and seeking enlightenment
And I left America and returned
To America with a family

And I worked with my Dad dabbling with
Opinions and politics and playing
With words believing it might be helpful
To mix Western and Eastern ideas

And much of my time is dedicated
To impartial justice and liberty
Because I understand that if freedom
Isn't defended tyrants will arise

And I also believe that greed anger
And ignorance are consuming poisons.

Before he died
Dad struggled and
mumbled to me
"I trust you to
keep me alive."

The dust is gathering on the books of
The shelves and some are books I've collected
But hundreds belonged to my Dad and there
Are the writings of Aristotle and

Bacon and the Common Book of Prayer and
Machiavelli and they are precious
With wisdom — and there are political
Books that time has rendered meaningless and

The paperback Westerns and detective
Adventures that diverted my Dad from
More serious reading — and in any
Of these thousands of bound pages I am

Likely to encounter the notes he wrote
In the margins revealing his presence.

The words are there
to read and consider
but I haven't the time
or inclination to
follow him.

The conversation happened thirty years
Ago and I don't recall what he said
Before or afterwards but I cherish
The words Zen Master Harada spoke to

Me as he said you need to trust yourself
And he cut across the differences
Of cultures and he appeared as solid
And settled as a mountain and the words

Are puzzling and without context but
Meaning emerges with the years that I
Needn't live in the oppositional
World where people struggle for attention —

Wholehearted effort is important and
There is a path opening before me.

A house is
commodious
in winter but
I want to be
at home anywhere.

Dad's
personality is
dispersed in
books
editorials
memory
words.

Snap Shots

I hold my possessions and remember
The memories they convey — and they are
A physical reality but they
Are also associated with a

Vanished world — my ex-wife is Japanese
And she has a shoebox of photos that
Were taken by her grandfather who was
A photographer with a platoon of

The Japanese Imperial Army
As he recorded the subjugation
Of China — my daughter began drawing
In grade school and she selected from the

Shoebox a tiny photo and drew a
Curious approximation of life.

I marvel at
the composure of
the Chinese man
seeing the
invaders.

The art colleges of America
Invite aspiring high school students
To an art fair in Minneapolis —
And in February of their senior

Year the students bring their artwork to show
The representatives from colleges — and
The parents and the students come to see
The quality of the art on offer —

And to see the representation of
The schools and to sample the various
Programs — and there is competition and
Nervousness among the students as if

Their worthiness depended completely
On the approval of their creations.

Jittery students
waiting in line and
glancing at the
competition are
busy comparing.

The pert voluptuous women and the
Dandy young men from the art colleges
Put on an exalted appearance as
They consider the line of supplicants

And they make suggestions for improvements
And they explain the advantages of
Their schools — and they take names and record their
Impressions of the encounters — and they

Don't really believe the pencil drawings
Done from photographs to be real artwork
Because the drawings are not creations
But are only copies of photos and

The authentic works of art must involve
Cultivated conceptual aplomb.

For years Jocelyn
was winning teenage
contests at county
and state fairs with
drawings of photos.

The fair was exciting and exhausting
And Jocelyn was torn between schools in
Alberta and Philadelphia but
Eventually she indulged her dream

And chose Moore College of Art and Design —
Not accounting for years of ensuing
Debt and the difficulty of finding
Employment after college — she painted

Portraits of models and fashioned a life-
Sized self-portrait in wire mesh and with an
An enormous canvas painted herself
Again using her feet — and it looks like

Brush work — and within a year in Philly
She met her future fiancé Eric.

Eric's a native
Philadelphian
and knows the gritty
metropolis.

We are the present manifestation
Of what came before us even if we
Don't know what happened before we came
Along and so we can't really gage how

Lucky or unfortunate we are — but
We can learn to see the landmarks on our
Way and become sensitive to the
Importance of being kind — even when

It's easy to get angry — my Dad was
An immigrant from Australia and I
Brought back a wife from Japan and now
Jocelyn is engaged to Eric whose

Family comes from Puerto Rico and who
Knows what happened hundreds of years ago?

Just a moment of
anger can twist the
direction of the
present
unpredictably.

Jocelyn was able to study at
Moore College of Art and Design because
Her grandmother Rema had carefully
Saved enough money and because Rema

Was generous and loving enough to
Pay for a large portion of tuition —
And after graduation Jocelyn
Was fortunate to paint the face of the

Famous broadcaster Ed Bradley and
And lucky to paint the players of the
76-ers Basketball team — and
These murals will brighten the buildings of

Philadelphia for decades to come
As real evidence of accomplishment.

Mural artists aren't
paid well and others
take the credit for their work
so Philadelphia
became depressing.

Leaving the classroom and entering the
Work force is disruptive and departing
From Philadelphia with Eric when
The ebb and flow of income became too

Unmanageable and returning to
Stillwater Minnesota was a shock —
Because Jocelyn and Eric had to
Accept the jobs with modest salaries

And stay with grandmother Rema — until
They could find better jobs and save money
And buy a car and get an apartment —
And now Jocelyn is painting when she

Can and she's working at the nursing home
Where her grandfather Angus passed away.

Jocelyn is
working with her mother
Yoshiko at the
nursing home as life is
spiraling from the past.

As Jocelyn's Dad
I'm helping when I
can but mostly
I'm observing.

— *Tekkan*

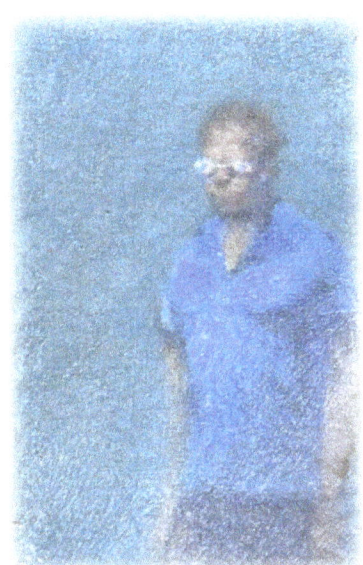

www.ingramcontent.com/pod-product-compliance
Lightning Source LLC
Chambersburg PA
CBHW042112100526
44587CB00025B/4023